## 2ND PLACE BOOK AWARD: 2022

## (BIOGRAPHY, AT-LARGE COMPETITION)

## NATIONAL FEDERATION OF PRESS WOMEN

"Every Daughter, or any woman who wants to be a Daughter should read Noel-Marie's book! You may know, or at least think you know, the basics about the Founders of the D.A.R. but now you can read the rest of the story about the strong, accomplished, tenacious, dedicated, committed, brave, independent, hardworking, don't-take-no-for-an-answer women."

— *Jane L. Johnson*

*Recording Secretary, Pleasant Prospect Chapter DAR;*
*Maryland National Defense State Chair;*
*former Maryland State Recording Secretary & Chapter Regent*

"The fascinating story of four women, who worked in 19th century Washington, D.C,. and who founded one of the largest women's volunteer organizations in the United States."

— *Susan Stonesifer*

*Historiographer, Episcopal Diocese of Washington*
*Ret. Branch Manager, Howard County Library System, MD*
*State Chaplain, District of Columbia DAR*

This advertisement in *The Washington Post*
on Aug. 17, 1890 was an important early step
by two of the four founders (Mary Desha
and Eugenia Washington) in establishing
the National Society of the Daughters of the
American Revolution.

# WOMEN OF VISION:

## *FOUNDERS*

## *OF THE*

## *DAUGHTERS OF THE*

## *AMERICAN REVOLUTION*

by

## Noël-Marie Fletcher

FLETCHER & CO. PUBLISHERS

*www.fletcherpublishers.com*

Women of Vision: Founders of the Daughters of the American
Revolution
Noël-Marie Fletcher
© December 2021, Fletcher & Co. Publishers LLC

Author: Noël-Marie Fletcher
Interior design & type: Noël-Marie Fletcher
Cover design: Zita Steele
Interior design: Noël-Marie Fletcher
Cover photo: Washington, D.C., votes for women parade in
1913 that Mary Smith Lockwood participated in and helped
organize, courtesy of the Washington, D.C. Public Library.
Cover paintings: Mary Smith Lockwood, Mary Desha, Ellen
Hardin Walworth and Eugenia Washington, courtesy of the
Daughters of the American Revolution.

Cataloging-in-Publication data for this book is available from
the Library of Congress.

Library of Congress Control Number: 2021952472


Cataloging information
ISBN-13 978-1-941184-38-7

First Edition
Published in the United States of America .

# Contents

The National Society of the Daughters of the American Revolution in Washington, D.C., circa 1915. Library of Congress.

Women visiting Washington, D.C. in 1896. Library of Congress.

# Acknowledgements

I would like to thank the National Society of the Daughters of the American Revolution, of which the author is a member, for permission to use images of paintings of the four founders for this book.

I'd also like to acknowledge the following for photo permissions and research information.

• Megan Klintworth, iconographer, Abraham Lincoln Presidential Library & Museum, Springfield, Ill.,

• University of Kentucky Special Collections and Research Center, Lexington, Ky.,

• James Parillo, Executive Director, The Saratoga Springs History Museum, N.Y., and

• Mark Zoeter, Library Assistant II, Local History/Special Collections, Alexandria Library, Va.

Street scene in Washington, D.C., circa 1889.
Library of Congress.

# The Founders

Few people experiencing the summer of 1890 would have thought that the world would become a better place thanks to a meeting of four strong women—a widowed single mother, a domestic-violence survivor, an impoverished Southern belle, and a poor relation of America's first president.

That year they came together in Washington, D.C., to found an enduring organization for women that would span the globe: the National Society of the Daughters of the American Revolution (DAR), an organization dedicated to promoting historic preservation, education, patriotism and remembrance of the legacy of Revolutionary War patriots.

Eugenia Washington, Mary Desha, Ellen Hardin Walworth and Mary Smith Lockwood, had all been dealt an unforeseen hand of misfortune in their private lives. They came from different walks to

Women trimming and stacking currency sheets in the Bureau of Engraving and Printing in Washington, D.C., (1890). Library of Congress.

9

Women operating machinery at the Bureau of Printing and Engraving in Washington, D.C., (1890). Library of Congress.

the nation's capital to earn a living for themselves, and, in some cases, also their children or parent.

"For those who are thrown unexpectedly on their own resources in part of the Union, Washington is the Mecca toward which their eyes naturally turn.

Widows of Union soldiers, daughters on whom the support of a mother and sisters devolves, 'grass' widows and maiden ladies compelled to self-support are all sheltered under one of the big government roofs," noted *The Washington Post* on May 14, 1891. The term "grass widows" was used then to describe women separated or divorced from husbands as well as single unmarried mothers.

The final decade of the 19th century was an important time for women seeking greater social reforms and the right to vote in a movement called "women's suffrage." After the Civil War, there were many displaced women throughout the United States. The nation had experienced a lengthy rebuilding during the Reconstruction Era (1865–1877) and improvements in civil rights following the abolishment of slavery. Women increasingly sought to expand their rights during a time when many had to fend for themselves and faced dilemmas

A teacher and her students on a field trip to the Library of Congress (1890). Library of Congress.

11

about how to find jobs.

It is important to understand life during the time period when DAR was founded to gain a better understanding about how truly remarkable these four women were. As older women, they became self-supporters against the odds. Under the title, *"Experiments in Wage-Earning,"* an article in *The Ladies' Home Journal* in March 1890 discussed this important topic, noting that the need to earn wages "falls most heavily" on women "who confront the dilemma after girlhood has passed." Well-educated women could try to teach, but faced obstacles if middle-aged. "Many a woman whose only available knowledge is housekeeping, turns to keeping a boarding or lodging house. But it takes considerable ability and shrewd calculation to make more than a living in this way, and involves hard work and constant anxiety. Some wish to become clerks, but retail employers generally prefer to put young and pretty girls behind their counters," it stated. "Fortunately, the range of choice avocations widens every years, and it seems to be generally accepted that a woman may do whatever she will."

When DAR was established in 1890, the youngest founder was Mary Desha at age 40, followed by Eugenia Washington (51). Both Mary Smith Lockwood and Ellen Hardin Walworth were 58 years old. Maverick women would be in the headlines including journalist Nellie Bly, suffragist Susan B. Anthony and attorney Belva Ann Lockwood,

Cyclist on steps of a 12th St. N.W. building in Washington, D.C., (1884). Library of Congress.

who had run twice for U.S. president in 1884 and 1888. Also that year, Benjamin Harrison was the 23rd President of the United States. Wyoming became the 44th state to join the union and the first state granting its women citizens the right to vote. Bicycles were the rage in cities like Washington, D.C., where the Washington Monument had been dedicated, the National Zoo opened and electric streetcars appeared. People

Nellie Bly (left), Susan B. Anthony (center), and Belva Lockwood (right), (1890). Library of Congress.

13

Hair styles in December 1889, *The Ladies' Home Journal.*

were reading Arthur Conan Doyle's first U.S. edition of *"A Study in Scarlet"*—in the first appearance of Sherlock Holmes. Home dressmaking was being replaced by ready-made clothes in shops. Princess-style evening gowns were a new craze for women along with updo hairstyles calling for hair to have side waves and be worn frizzed in front. Fashion demanded that dresses having matching colored leather shoes (ranging from $10 to $15 a pair) for men, women, children and infants, noted the *New York Evening Sun.*

Patriotic fervor increased in America after the nation celebrated its first centennial in Philadelphia in 1876 and again in early 1889 while preparing for a centennial celebration in New York City for George Washington's Inauguration. Remembering colonial history, people formed patriotic organizations. The Sons of the American Revolution (SAR) was established in 1889. After it voted in April 1890 to exclude women, Mary Smith Lockwood wrote a letter to *The Washington Post* in July 1890 about a patriotic woman named Hannah White Arnett (1733–1823), who supported the Revolutionary War and prevented a group of men in her presence in New Jersey from backing the British. Lockwood ended her letter with: *"Where will the Sons and Daughters of the American Revolution place Hannah Arnett?"* A few days letter, a great-grandson of Hannah named William Osborne McDowell, also a founder of SAR, wrote a reply to the newspaper calling for women to form their own group and offering to help. Both of these letters spurred the four bold women into action that led to the establishment of DAR.

William Osborne McDowel. Wikimedia Commons.

An announcement about the purpose of the society and eligibility requirements was published in *The Washington Post* on Aug. 17, 1890 in a notice penned by Mary Desha and signed by Miss Eugenia Washington as registrar. The purpose of the new organization was to:

- Gather materials for history,
- Preserve Revolutionary War artifacts,
- Study the history of that time period, and
- Determine how best to remember patriot ancestors and celebrate their achievements.

Noting the importance to specifically preserve records about the historic deeds of patriotic women, she listed membership eligibility requirements as

Caroline Scott Harrison, wife of President Harrison. Library of Congress.

lineal descent from "an ancestor who assisted in establishing the American Independence during the War of the Revolution." Applicants were instructed to submit their information to her at 813 13th St. in Washington, D.C. On Oct. 11, 1890, the DAR was formally organized in a meeting at the home of Mary S. Lockwood at The Strathmore Arms. The first president general was Mrs. Benjamin Harrison (First Lady and wife of the President). The four founders joined the Executive Committee and took the following offices:

• Mary Desha as one of the vice presidents general,

• Ellen Hardin Walworth among the secretaries general,

• Eugenia Washington among the registrars,

• Mary Smith Lockwood as historian.

Not only did they pay from their own pockets for initial startup expenses, the founders also were instrumental in all ground-breaking aspects of the DAR.

Mary Smith Lockwood proposed the organization obtain a location and later a fireproof building to

16

Photo of a golden spinning wheel with a distaff of silver flax in the DAR insignia. It was designed in 1891 by Dr. George Brown Goode, below, a Smithsonian museum administrator and zoologist. Library of Congress.

hold historical documents and artifacts. Also Mary Desha suggested that assistance be given to the Mary Washington Association after her grave was put up for auction despite her being the mother of George Washington. Both Eugenia Washington and Mary Desha were among those who signed the Act of Incorporation.

On June 8, 1891, the National Society of the Daughters of the American Revolution was incorporated under an act of the U.S. Congress.

Dr. Goode's ancestors were colonial founders of Connecticut, Massachusetts, New Jersey and Virginia. He was a member of SAR. Wikimedia Commons.

17

Portrait of Eugenia Washington by Edith
Harrison Loop. It was presented April 21,
1916 to DAR as a gift from 187 chapters and
individuals. Born in New York City to both
parents who were painters, the artist was
a portrait painter who lived in California.
Image courtesy of DAR.

# Chapter 1: Eugenia Washington

Being brave, independent and hardworking defined Eugenia Scholay Washington—great-grandniece of President George Washington, whom she resembled.

Known to her friends as Miss Eugie, she was uncomfortable when she attracted attention due to her blueblood relatives.

When permission was sought to write about her life story, she replied: "I was taught that a woman's name should appear in print but twice, when she married and when she died, and I have no desire to bring myself before the public." Eugie was the great-granddaughter of Col. Samuel Washington (brother of George Washington). Col. Washington (born in 1734) served with Virginia forces during Revolutionary War and was a younger sibling of George Washington. Samuel suffered from

George Washington family Coat of Arms. Family motto: *Exitus acta probat.* (The outcome is the test of the act.) Wikimedia Commons.

Portrait of Col. Samuel Washington by
James Alexander Simpson (1855). George
Washington's Mount Vernon.

tuberculous and died of a respiratory ailment at age
46 in 1781 only three weeks before the victory by
the Continental Army/French Army at Yorktown,
Va. Her father William Temple Washington married
Margaret Calhoun Fletcher in 1831 in Lexington, Ky.

Margaret was a descendant of Col. Charles François Joseph, Count de Flechir, a French nobleman (1755–1815) who came with the Marquis de Lafayette to America and served as a private and later captain in the Revolutionary War.

"She [Eugie] had the courage of her convictions and nothing could swerve her from the course she deemed right," wrote Letitia Green Stevenson, in 1913. "She would willingly have sacrificed life, and all that she held most dear, for a settled principle."

Keeping with her desire for privacy, Eugie made no public outcry when she—among the few living close blood relatives to George Washington—was not invited to a fancy New York City gala in 1899 celebrating the first president's inauguration. Instead the Washington family was primarily represented by relatives of his wife Martha. One newspaper declared: "Not a Washington of Washington was invited…"

Another stated: "Some surprise has been expressed that Miss Eugenia Washington will not be present at the Washington centennial celebration in New York. This is the reason: Miss Washington is in the first

HISTORICAL REGISTER
OF

Officers of the Continental Army

DURING THE

WAR OF THE REVOLUTION,

April, 1775, to December, 1783.

Flechir, Charles Francois Joseph Count de. Colonel of Horse, en second, 13th April, 1780; gallant conduct at York; distinguished conduct at St. Christopher, where, with a small body of 300 Grenadiers and Chasseurs he repulsed and routed 1400 troops the British had landed; served from 1760; Captain, 7th June, 1776; Colonel of Horse, en second, 13th April, 1780.

assistant postmaster-general's office, Post Office department, and is too poor to grace social events in New York, but not too depressed to be keenly alive to the honor of her great kinsman, whose name she bears with dignity and self-respecting pride." The Washington, D.C., *Evening Star* on April

Eugie's boss. Don M. Dickson, Postmaster General, 1887–1889. Library of Congress.

18, 1889 went on to describe her humble situation. Learning that she had fallen on hard times after the Civil War, Gen. Ulysses S. Grant "felt it not only a duty, but a pleasure" to give her that job in the Post Office. "Her only wish is to remain undisturbed in her position and let those who are financially able do her kinsman honor," the newspaper noted.

It is unknown why she did not to marry when society opened its doors to her in Washington, D.C., a locale abundant with powerful men of means. She chose a single life of self-support and sacrifice.

She was born June 27, 1838 in the family home called Megwillie (a combination of her parent's names). It was located about 10 miles from Harper's

Ferry in present-day West Virginia in what had been part of her grandfather George Steptoe Washington's Harewood estate. Raised and educated by President Washington, her grandfather was one of the five nephews named by Washington as executors of his will, which

George Steptoe Washington (1771–1809), by John Drinker. Wikimedia Commons.

bequeathed one of his swords to each nephew.

Eugie was the second-youngest after her brother Ferdinand Steptoe Washington (1843–1912). Her surviving siblings were elder sisters Millissent Fowler Washington McPherson (1824–1893) and Jean Charlotte Washington Moncure (1834–1916).

A Missouri newspaper described her father William Temple Washington in 1863 as remarkable, "a tall man, reticent, grave, very much resembling the father of this country." Her father attended the College of William & Mary and was also said to have graduated from Transylvania University in Lexington, Ky. Described as an intellectual bookworm, he decided to homeschool his children. Eugie's father was "a gentleman of literary and quiet tastes." It is a testament to her intelligence and good education at home that she not only made a successful career as a government clerk, but also cofounded DAR and filled a key role requiring attention to detail as a registrar for new members.

"While the young girl, Eugenia, had careful intellectual training, she also enjoyed the free and cheerful life characteristic of the old Virginia home: every day she was in the saddle galloping over the beautiful hillsides of her native state, and in the evening she entered into the family and social intercourse of an agreeable neighborhood," a DAR article noted.

A few years before the outbreak of the Civil War, her father moved the family to a plantation in Falmouth, Stafford County, Va. It was across the Rappahannock River opposite the port town of Fredericksburg. This move had dire consequences for their family. The 1860 U.S. census for Stafford showed the family consisting of her 59-year-old father, whose profession was listed as a farmer, her mother (age 54), a sister Jane (26), Eugenia (21) and brother Steptoe (17), also listed as a farmer.

During the 19th century, the river provided important hydropower for manufacturing flour and

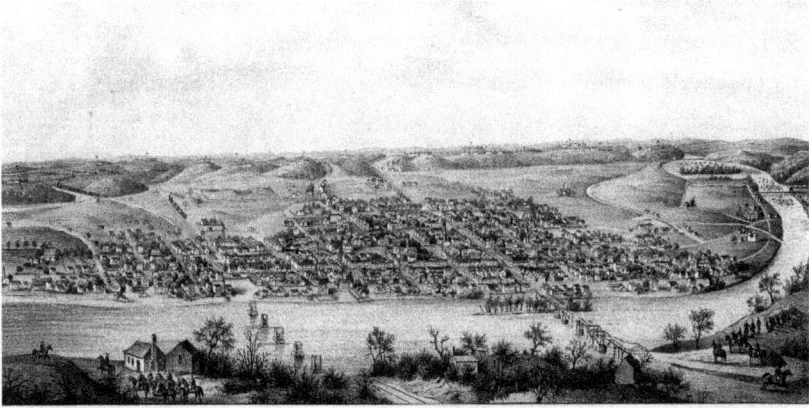

View in November 1862 of Fredericksburg, Va., opposite the Rappahannock River. Eugie's family lived in Falmouth, shown at the bottom of the illustration. Library of Congress.

textiles. It also occupied a strategic location, with a network of roads and railroad between Richmond and Washington, D.C. The Fredericksburg docks were frequented by steamboats traveling to and from Baltimore and Alexandria.

As the fabric of the country was ripped apart over the issue of slavery, the Washington family, like many others, became caught in the deadly struggles. Although Eugie's father William Temple Washington was opposed to Secession and one of the few men in his area to vote against it, he would not break with Virginia when it left the Union to become one of the Confederate States of America. Their home soon fell under Union control after the Army first arrived in the Fredericksburg area in the spring of 1862. Civilian movements were

Camp of 110th Pennsylvania Infantry near Falmouth, Va., in December 1862 (above). Union soldiers entrenched along the west bank of the Rappahannock River at Fredericksburg in early 1863. These type of sights would have been familiar to Eugie. Library of Congress.

restricted. Mail was intercepted during a four-month occupation. The Union army staged three major campaigns across the Rappahannock River

Post Office at Headquarters Army of Potomac in Falmouth(April 1863). Notice the women on the left and far right. Library of Congress.

near Fredericksburg that resulted in four battles—Fredericksburg, Chancellorsville, Wilderness and Spotsylvania Court House—in which over 105,000 men died, were wounded or went missing.

Unlike other residents, Eugie and her family harbored no hostility to Yankee soldiers. Her niece Eugenia Moncure Bradfield, related how for nearly nine months, Union Gen. Winfield Scott Hancock was encamped near Eugie's front yard. "He was always extremely courteous to them and took a great interest in the young Eugenia."

The ties between Eugie and Gen. Hancock (who commanded one of the Army of the Potomac's best divisions) grew stronger during the Battle of

Fredericksburg on Dec. 13, 1862. She would find herself caught in one of the most vicious and deadly battles during the Civil War. Although her mother was alive at that time, her whereabouts are unknown. (Margaret died at age 58 in January 1865, four months before Gen. Lee surrendered at Appomattox Court House. She was buried in Falmouth.)

Gen. Winfield Scott Hancock during the Civil War. Library of Congress.

Near Falmouth in January 1863 drawn then Alfred R. Waud. Library of Congress.

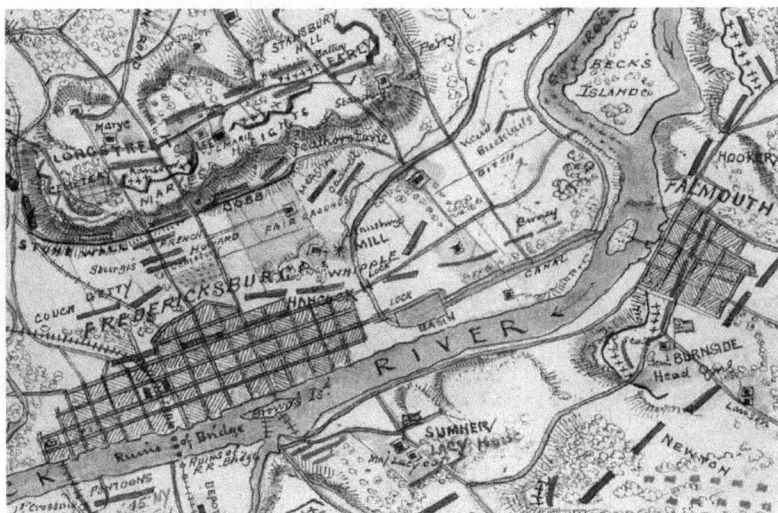

Close up map of the Plan for the Battle of Fredericksburg, Va., on Dec. 13, 1862. It shows the area around Fredericksburg, including Marye's Heights outside the city and Falmouth across the Rappahannock River. Library of Congress.

To prepare for the battle, the Union Army sent thousands of troops to bombard the Fredericksburg area on Dec. 11, 1862. The next day they occupied the area. Soldiers slept in streets, and entered homes and shops to loot. The town became the first sizeable American city to be plundered by Americans during the Civil War. (Area residents who escaped to avoid danger returned to find they had lost almost everything.)

War had brought devastation to the Washington family home at Falmouth. Union soldiers were described as quartered in large numbers throughout the property, bringing so much activity that one

Above: Ruins of Phillips House near Falmouth during the Civil War. Below: Company I, of the 6th Pennsylvania Cavalry in Falmouth (June 1863). Library of Congress.

perimeter of his land became a heavily trafficked road. The Union army encampment across the Rappahannock River at Falmouth gave officers a clear view of both Fredericksburg as well as Rebel troops.

On the evening of Dec. 12 skirmishes began, leaving many wounded soldiers. Although seeking to escape the area with her father (partially paralyzed from a stroke) before the main battle began, Eugie stayed overnight to treat the injured. Her plan was to leave after daybreak the morning of the decisive battle. That day was described by a war correspondent from *The New York Times* as "mild and balmy as a September day, though the mist and fog of a late Indian summer hung over the field of battle."

Near Fredericksburg, Union forces planned a two-pronged attack against the Confederate forces of Gen. Robert E. Lee in a bid to attack Richmond. However, the Union Army experienced one of its most crushing defeats. Delays in getting a pontoon bridge ready for crossing the Rappahannock River enabled Lee's Army to position his men on high ground with good cover opposite Fredericksburg where the Federals were pinned down. Confederates pounded

Gen. Robert E. Lee in uniform riding his gray horse, Traveller, during the Civil War. He rode the horse, known for its bravery, in many battles. Library of Congress.

Union soldiers with bursts from two long-range cannons (12-pound Whitworth rifles able to fire distinctive shells more than two

Whitworth gun captured from Confederates near Richmond in 1865. Library of Congress.

miles). Damage sustained to Martha Stephen's house indicates just how fierce the fighting was. The house—where Confederate sharpshooters fired from windows and the roof—was hit by mortars and had more than 1,000 bullet holes in it.

One Union attack focused on Marye's Heights where Gen. Hancock led his division. There Confederates also had better positioning not only on top of the hill but with a line of artillery firing from behind a thick stone wall (next to Sunken Road) at the base of Marye's Heights, which rose 600 yards beyond Fredericksburg. Rebel soldiers, looking downward, turned the open slopes around Fredericksburg into a killing field. The thoroughfare next to Sunken Road, beaten down by wagons wheels, served as a trench for the Confederates.

Gen. Andrew A. Humphreys' charge at the head of his division after sunset Dec. 13, 1862, drawn then by Alfred R. Waud. Library of Congress.

Eugie's flight to safety didn't go as planned. When she left with her father "the roads were choked with reserves and supplies, the artillery was in position, and before she could make her way through, she was caught on the battlefield in the very center of the most hotly contested objective. The only shelter the soldiers could point out to the young girl and her charge was the furrow left by a cannon which was already in action. She placed her father next to the scant wall of earth and lay with her own body between him and the rain of death. Lying on that dreadful field, she witnessed the whole battle and saw brigade after brigade broken or wiped out in the fierce charges. All through the day she waited for the battle to end and the hour to come when

Fredericksburg, Dec. 13, 1862: Charge of 114th Pennsylvania Volunteers, Collis' Zouaves to the rescue of Randolph's Rhode Island Battery, by Carl Rochling (1865). Photo: Noël-Marie Fletcher.

she could convey her father to safety," according to *American Monthly Magazine* in 1906.

"Oh! It was a terrible day. The destruction of life had been fearful, and nothing was gained... Irish blood and Irish bones covered that terrible field to-day...We are slaughtered like sheep and no result but defeat," wrote Capt. William B. Nagle, 88th New York Infantry, in a letter to his father. The Irish Brigade attacked Marye's Heights with 1,250 men, losing 44% in a single hour. Every officer of the 69th New York who went in ended up dead.

On a plain, nearly half a mile wide, between the town's suburbs and the first ridge of hills, "our brave troops surged and swept, forward and backward, in the tide of battle, for 10 long hours," wrote *The New York Times.* "The day was lost! Our men retired. Immediately cannon and musketry ceased their roar, and in a moment of silence death succeeded the stormy fury of 10 hours battle."

A Confederate survivor of the Battle of Fredericksburg, Capt. David Gregg McIntosh stated: "The worst ordeal the soldier had to encounter is to lie still, and do nothing under heavy fire. It will get on his nerves, if he had to keep it up over long."

It is impossible to fully comprehend what Eugie and her father experienced that day—as well as any type of post-traumatic stress they, as civilians, may have endured in such a horrific situation. "Artillery caused only

Stone wall at Marye's Heights 20 minutes after it was stormed in another battle in May 1863. Library of Congress.

about 8% of the casualties on a Civil War battlefield, but its presence had a powerful psychological effect on men. The boom of dozens of cannon, the explosion of shells, the whizzing of shell fragments and the sound as they ripped into the ground were a torment few men forgot. Booming artillery and exploding shells created chaos and terror," noted a National Park Service display at the Fredericksburg Battlefield Visitor Center.

It is evident that this experience never left Eugie since she told several women at DAR about it. One DAR acquaintance named Ella Loraine Dorsey stated in 1915 that Eugie "saw regiments destroyed and brigades wiped out in the five terrible charges across the plain, where even the Irish barely reached and touched in the dying in that wall of death; and when the battle was over, she had to suffer sights and sounds no woman should be required to endure....terrible as the scene was, she had to witness far worse at the end of the war. On that field she had seen but dead bodies and heard the agony of wounded men, but after the war the field of desolation she saw was a whole section of our country—industrially wrecked, filled with mourning hearts, ruined homes, broken fortunes, crushed hopes and the anguish of defeat."

It is said that Eugie helped care for Gen. Hancock, who suffered minor injuries that day despite having a close brush with death. Gen. Hancock wrote the

Destroyed homes in Fredericksburg. Library of Congress.

following to his wife Almira. "We went into action to-day but did not gain the works we sought, although we held all the positions we gained. I had three of my staff wounded yesterday and four of their horses killed. I had one bullet through my overcoat, just escaping my abdomen; one-half inch more and I would have had a fatal wound. Out of the 5,700 men I carried into action, I have this morning in line but 1,450. Out of 17 regiments of my command, there are but three or four commanders who are not killed or wounded. In one regiment two officers are left. In one brigade the general officers and all the field officers, except one, in six regiments were killed or wounded. It was a desperate undertaking, and the army fought hard," from *"Reminiscences of Winfield Scott Hancock"* by Almira Russell Hancock (1887).

After the war, Gen. Hancock repaid Eugie by taking an interest in her welfare. She was alone and caring for her father while in great financial distress, as were most Southern families. Gen. Hancock used his influence with Union leaders to get her a government job in Washington, D.C., so she could support herself and father, as retold by her niece Eugenia Moncure Bradfield.

She moved to the nation's capital in 1867 from her family home, which had been left ravaged by the destruction of war. Both of her

**EUGENIA WASHINGTON.**

News illustration in *The Times* (Philadelphia) 1899.

sisters were married. She took it upon herself to care for her father and provide financial support.

City directories throughout the rest of her life listed her occupation as a government clerk. In 1869 she lived at 486 E. Street. In 1878, she relocated to 13th St. N.W., eventually moving to 813 13th St. N.W. where she lived for the rest of her life with a married couple, who were two longtime Washington family servants, a few blocks away from the White House.

"If she has the characteristic modesty of her family, she has also the family courage that does not shrink from any plain duty," according to a description of her in a DAR magazine article.

Fighting poverty, she apparently petitioned Congress on July 15, 1867 with an offer to sell a sword in her possession that had belonged to George Washington. The fate of this sword is unknown, as well as whether she was able to raise funds from its sale. Before her father's death in April 1877, he sold one of George Washington's swords to George Riggs, a Washington, D.C., banker. "In consequence, it is thought, of pecuniary

One of George Washington's swords at the National Museum of American History. Photo: Noël-Marie Fletcher.

embarrassments, due doubtless largely to the vicissitudes of war, Mr. Washington parted with this sword," which was known as the George Steptoe Washington sword. It was later donated by the Riggs family to Mount Vernon, according to a book published in 1894.

Eugie's experiences during the Civil War led her to see herself as a peacemaker healing wounds between people. Those who knew Eugie recall her saying because of the widespread terror and sorrows caused by the war, she believed it would be good to create a national organization to unite people in a common purpose. This motivation led to her becoming a founder of DAR and work for the group for the rest of her life. She became a devout Catholic after visiting a relative in Louisiana after the war. She regularly attended St. Matthew's Church, founded in D.C. in 1840.

After entering the government system, Eugie found herself among other descendants of patriots working to make ends meet. "There the standing of the ladies who work in the departments, unlike the self-supporting women of other cities, is not affected in the least by their position as employees of the Government," noted *The Washington Post* in May 1891. "On the contrary, here are to be found some of the bluest blood of our native land. Compelled, as many are, by some unlucky stroke of fortune, to seek their own bread, they bravely fight their own battle, often supporting their children or their mother in some distant country home." Among these were a relative of Patrick Henry and a great-granddaughter of Benjamin Franklin named Ellen Abert who worked in the Department of Justice.

Women visit an art gallery in Washington, D.C. (circa 1899). Library of Congress.

In Washington, D.C., Eugie's name appeared sporadically as she attended society events. She was mentioned among the visitors to the White House on June 30, 1881 when James Garfield was president. For the most part, she led a quiet and private life. A DAR article said Eugie "was especially domestic in her taste, fond of housekeeping, reading and fancy work, and, as she said, 'never so happy as in my own home—when blessed with one.'"

During the summer of 1890, she put her energy into founding DAR. She was assigned National Number 1 in the new organization, where she became registrar. "The position of Registrar was an arduous one, but she was untiring in her exertions to secure accurate and reliable proofs of all statements to be placed on the records of the Society in connection with the applications for membership," noted DAR.

A few months after DAR was organized, Eugie met prospective member Janet E.H. Richards. In December 1890, "my membership papers were accepted and filed by our first Registrar, Miss Eugenia Washington, who had remarked to me after scanning my historic references, 'I wish all applications were as clear and authentic as these. It would certainly save me a whole heap of trouble!' This gratifying word of commendation is my earliest memory of our rather spicy first Registrar," Janet recalled in 1940.

Despite suffering from serious eye ailments, Eugie continued working hard for DAR. She was among the charter members of the Dolley Madison Chapter in D.C. She transferred her membership in 1899 to the George Washington Chapter in Galveston, Texas, and became one of four members of the Washington family to belong to that chapter.

Having poor health for some time, Eugie refused to slow down although her

```
Washington Eugenia, ck, 813 13th nw
Washington Fannie, 1704 L nw
Washington Fanny, domestic, 1301 Clifton
    nw
WASHINGTON FLORAL CO, Otto
    Bauer, manager, violets a spe-
    cialty, 717 15th nw, tel 2008
```

Top line: Eugie's residential listing in the Washington, D.C. city directory for 1899.

doctor told her she was overworked. She refused to take time away from her government job until so could no longer avoid it—only staying at home to rest for one week before her death. Eugie died on Thanksgiving Day, Nov. 30, 1900. Newspapers throughout the United States and even in England printed her obituary. Some even said she died "in comparative poverty" with only a servant at her side.

A simple funeral service was conducted at the home of her sister and brother-in-law Thomas Moncure at 305 B St. N.E. in Washington, D.C.

Eugie's photo and signature in DAR's *American Monthly Magazine* in 1892.

Floral arrangements included a magnificent wreath sent by DAR—four-foot-high, with white roses, chrysanthemums, violets and palms. Cofounder Mary Desha sent white roses tied with a white satin ribbon. She was buried beside her parents' graves in Falmouth, Va. Friends from Fredericksburg were pallbearers. Two of her nieces traveled with her remains, and local DAR chapters met the funeral party. She was laid to rest near the shores of the Rappahannock River.

After Eugie's death, another DAR cofounder Ellen Hardin Walworth penned a newspaper letter. "She labored for the society from its beginning until

## FOUNDER OF D. A. R. DEAD

Sudden End of Miss Eugenia Washington in This City.

Was Great Grand-niece of Gen. Washington—Long Employed in the Post-office and Pension Office—Funeral to Be Held To-morrow.

Miss Eugenia Washington, a great-grand niece of the Father of His Country, and the founder and one of the honorary vice presidents general of the Daughters of the American Revolution, and president of the Society of Founders and Patriots, died suddenly about 4 o'clock yesterday morning at her home, 813 Thirteenth street northwest. She held a clerical position at the Post-office Department, and although she had been complaining a long time, friends were unable to persuade her to relinquish her duties. She was at work Wednesday, but complained of feeling ill that night. She was somewhat better Thursday, but her condition became worse toward evening, and at 10 o'clock hemorrhages of the heart began, continuing until the end came.

Mrs. Jane Washington Moncure, of 305 B street northeast, sole surviving member of the immediate family, and a sister of the deceased, was immediately notified and directed that the remains be removed to the residence of the former. The funeral will take place at 11 o'clock to-morrow morning from the home of Mrs. Moncure. Interment will be made at Fredericksburg, Va. The local organization of the Society of the Daughters of the American Revolution is requested to assemble at the Pennsylvania station at 10:30 o'clock to-morrow as a mark of respect. The remains will be taken to Virginia on the train which will leave at 10:55 o'clock.

Miss Washington was a native of Jefferson County, now West Virginia, having been born there sixty years ago. William Temple Washington, her father, was a grandson of Col. Samuel Washington, brother of Gen. George Washington. Her mother, Margaret Calhoun Fletcher, was a daughter of Gen. Thomas Fletcher, a member of the staff of Gen. William Henry Harrison during the War of 1812. The deceased was a descendant, on the maternal side, of the Count de Fiechir, who came to this country with the Marquis de Lafayette, his kinsman, and rose from a private in the ranks to the position of captain in the Continental Army.

Miss Washington came to this city in 1867, and was appointed to a clerkship in the Patent Office through the influence of Gen. W. S. Hancock. She conceived the necessity and propriety of forming a society to perpetuate the historical associations and ideals of, as well as the events connected with, the Revolutionary period. While Mrs. Ellen Hardin Wadsworth, of New York, and Miss Mary Desha, of this city, shared with Miss Washington the honor of having founded the society, the latter cherished and developed her ideal long before the organization was really formed in 1896, and is justly credited with the origination of the society.

*The Washington Post* on Dec. 1, 1900.

*The Evening Star* (Washington, D.C.), Dec. 3, 1900.

the day of her death." It noted that Eugie's passing "will be a matter of regret to all who knew this splendid, clever woman."

Her efforts helped the DAR to grow into a thriving organization whose members numbered nearly 30,000 women at that time.

Portrait of Mary Desha painted in 1914 by
Aline E. Solomons, a Washington, D.C.
artist (who also held leadership positions
in DAR). The painting was presented to the
national society by what is now the Col. John
Washington-Katherine Montgomery Chapter
in Washington, D.C. Image courtesy of DAR.

# Chapter 2: Mary Desha

Despite a family history of tragedies, Mary Desha was a spunky, single Southern belle who drew inspiration from patriotic ancestors to fight for women's rights and lead volunteer organizations.

She was born in Lexington, Ky., in 1850 in a county named after the Marquis de Lafayette , the French hero of the Revolutionary War. The Desha (pronounced Deshay) family was of French Huguenot ancestry. Her family was close-knit, with many prominent members, who were well aware of the history of their patriotic ancestors and those whose who fought in the Revolutionary War. Her grandfather Gen. Joseph Desha, well-known for his military service in the War of 1812, was the 9th Governor of Kentucky.

In fact, Gen. Desha spent time with the famous Lafayette during a year-long, 24-state tour. In the grand procession into Lexington, Gov. Desha followed immediately after Lafayette as they entered the city in an open, four-wheeled

Portrait of Gen. Joseph Desha by Katherine Helm (1908). Public domain.

barouche carriage drawn by bay horses. "Probably the grandest gathering ever seen in Lexington was the occasion of the reception of Gen. Lafayette, May 16, 1825. In no place in this country did the old hero receive a more cordial welcome than in the seat of the country which was named in his honor. An immense concourse of people from all parts of Kentucky and from several other states, companies of infantry, artillery, and cavalry, Revolutionary soldiers, distinguished strangers, members of all profession, went out to meet him, wearing 'Lafayette badges,'" according to the *"History of Lexington, Kentucky"* by George Washington Ranck (1872).

Mary's grandmother (Margaret Bledsoe Desha) was known for spinning flax and weaving it into fine linen clothing worn by her husband in public office when he served in both

U.S. Capitol and Pennsylvania Avenue in Washington, D.C. before 1814 by Benjamin Henry Latrobe (1810). Mary's grandfather served in the U.S. House of Representatives for six terms (1768-1842). Library of Congress.

branches of the state legislature and six terms as a representative to Congress. This family union produced 13 children, who became leading figures in Kentucky history in public, military and patriotic endeavors.

Despite their high status, the family was embroiled in scandal due to a sensational murder. Gen. Desha's son Isaac Bledsoe was convicted of slaying and robbing a traveler named Francis Baker. The killing happened in 1824 when Baker, a magazine editor, journeyed from his home in Mississippi to marry his sweetheart in New Jersey. Baker met Isaac at a tavern.

Isaac Desha, the person apprehended in Mason county for the murder and highway robbery of FRANCIS BAKER, has been arraigned before an examining Court, and after a minute investigation of the testimony, remanded to jail to be tried at the next term of Fleming Circuit Court. The examination of witnesses continued three days. The prisoner was defended by Messrs TAUL and CRAWFORD;—the prosecution was conducted by MARTIN MARSHALL, Attorney for the Commonwealth.

*Kentucky Reporter,* Nov. 29, 1824.

Isaac offered to ride with Baker to provide directions. Two hours later, Isaac was seen with bloodstains on his clothing and in possession of Baker's horse, saddlebags and belongings. Due to his behavior at the time, Isaacs's pregnant wife left him. A jury convicted Isaac twice of murder and sentenced him to hang despite his father being Gen. Desha. Before the execution, Isaac slit his throat in an attempted suicide. He survived and his windpipe was repaired with a silver tube.

Afterwards, Gen. Desha pardoned his son, who left for Texas under an assumed name. Partially identified by the silver tube in his throat, Isaac was arrested again for robbing and killing another man. Isaac admitted

A main building of Transylvania University when Dr. Desha attended. The building was constructed in 1818 and burned in 1829. From *"History of Higher Education in Kentucky"* by Alvin Fayette Lewis (1899).

guilt in both murders while incarcerated. Before that trial began, he died of a fever in 1828 at age 26. His younger brother was Dr. John Randolph Desha—Mary's father.

In contrast to his violent sibling, John Randolph Desha started a quiet career as a physician. He graduated from Transylvania University in 1827 as a doctor of medicine, specializing in "epidemic fever."

Eleven years later, he married Mary Bracken Curry. The hand of death was not far behind and would claim three of their five children: their eldest and only son Ben died at age 14 in 1841, while

50

Adelaide (Adda) 15 and Ella (8) both died sometime after July 1860. It is unknown what caused their deaths. The only surviving children were Mary (known as Molly) and her older sister Issa, the eldest by seven years.

In April 1860, Dr. Desha was appointed in medical manager of the Eastern Kentucky Lunatic Asylum, which had been stricken by cholera and smallpox. The asylum, converted from a hospital, was the state's first such institution. Dr. Desha apparently kept his affiliation with it for several years, with his name appearing with it in 1869 and 1871.

Despite personal tragedies, Dr. Desha's family prospered. He won a Premium (1st place) prize at the 7th Annual Exhibition of Kentucky Agricultural and Mechanical Association fair for having the best pair of carriage horses in 1857 in the carriage/buggy horses' category. Lexington was known as a jewel in the South—famed for its horses, having twice the number of

Horses in a field in Lexington, Ky. (circa 1900). Lexington Public Library.

carriages of any similar American city. It was a hub of literary culture and education. The family seemed to live a comfortable life. In the U.S. Census for 1860, Dr. Desha listed the value of his real estate and $6,000 and personal estate at $22,000. The family home was surrounded by neighbors of a similar social standing — two lawyers, a photojournalist, a dry goods merchant, an insurance agent, a watchmaker and a flour merchant.

The Desha family experienced tumult throughout the Civil War. At first, Kentucky took neither side, issuing

Mary Desha at age 15, in *The American Monthly Magazine*, August 1911.

a proclamation of state neutrality in the spring of 1861. Twice as many Kentuckians joined the Union Army compared to those who took the Confederate side. In 1862, the state asked the Federals for assistance after a failed Confederate invasion, and Kentucky became a Union state.

Mary's uncle Lucius Junius Brutus Desha, who had a large plantation, was a politician and Rebel sympathizer serving in the General Assembly for Harrison County. He was arrested by the Federals in July 1862 as a civilian suspected of supporting the Confederate cause and imprisoned in Camp Chase, Ohio. (Tried for treason and acquitted, he was called Gen. Lucius for past service in the Kentucky Militia.) Lucius was among 60 private citizens in that county arrested by Union soldiers for disloyalty and confined in military prisons. Lucius was said to have taken no part in the armed action against the Union, but was viewed as a potential danger for his views.

WILLIAMS'

LEXINGTON CITY DIRECTORY.

FOR 1864-5.

TO WHICH IS APPENDED A

UNITED STATES POST OFFICE DIRECTORY.

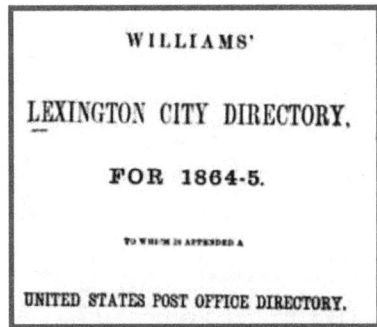

Desha John R. phys h n w c High and Upper

It appears Dr. Desha didn't serve in the military during the war. He is listed in the Lexington city directory for 1864 as a town physician. However, there are a few accounts stating that both Issa and Mary were nurses during the Civil War. The sisters in their later lives assisted former Confederates and other veterans. In September 1861, Issa at the age of 18 married William Campbell Preston (C.P.) Breckinridge, who served as a Confederate officer.

One of Mary's cousins Capt. Joseph (Jo) Desha, son of Gen. Lucius, served on the Rebel side with the 9th Kentucky Mounted Infantry and achieved fame twice. The first was during the Civil War when he was carted away on a battlefield as dead when hit in the head by a cannonball shell at Murfreesboro. After a dressing was applied to his head injury, Capt. Desha returned to his troops. Apparently, Confederate President Davis asked to be introduced afterwards to the only many who ever survived being struck in the head by a cannonball. His

Mary's cousin Joseph (Jo) Desha (1833–1902) survived a cannonball wound to the head, but lost the use of an arm.

name again appeared in the press for being in one of the last duels in Kentucky history. In 1866, the former Confederate officer met with a childhood acquaintance Capt. Alec Kimbrough, a former Union soldier, on a farm for a duel despite the fact that it was illegal. Their dispute was caused by an unspecified personal matter that happened before the war. Both men went into a field and missed each other with the first shots fired. Then Capt. Desha shot Kimbrough through the right hip, causing him to walk with a permanent limp thereafter. The two fled to Canada to escape justice. They were both pardoned in 1875.

An interesting view of Mary has given in 1940 by a DAR member who knew her. "Because as a Southern girl, who had lived through the excitement of the War between the States and the humiliation of defeat, I was surprised at her devotion to the United States Flag. When I asked her about it, her reply was as surprising as it was characteristic. 'Soon after the close of the War,' she said, 'I went to teaching school, and because my ancestors had fought under Old Glory in the American Revolution, I considered the Stars and Stripes as much my flag as the flag of the North. I therefore gave a small flag to every child in my school, and at a certain hour each day we had a little ceremony, when at a signal each child opened her desk and produced her flag and proceeded to wave it, while we sang a patriotic verse,'" recalled Janet E.H. Richards. "I can still see the snappy gleam in her dark eyes and hear her merry laugh as I expressed my surprise and pleasure in this story."

Undoubtedly times were difficult for Mary's family after the Civil War. Kentucky was primarily a state where nearly 90% of all farms were small (between 20 and 50 acres) rather than large plantations typical in other Southern states. The climate was unsuitable for growing cotton and

An industrial exposition in 1872 in Lexington, Ky., illustrated then. Library of Congress.

rice. Instead small farms mainly produced livestock, flour and tobacco. There was social and political upheaval during the Reconstruction era. It has been stated that hardships stemming from the Civil War forced Mary and her mother to go into teaching to earn a living. However, there is little evidence for this. The U.S. Census for 1870 lists Dr. Desha (age 66) as a physician, his 50-year-old wife's occupation as keeping house, and Mary (aged 20 and called Mollie) with neither the occupation of a teacher nor student. (Issa was already married.) In fact, Dr. Desha was still listed on the board of managers in 1871 at the state-run Lunatic Asylum. Evidently he still had some income from the state government. Dr. Desha is also referred to as Covington Medical Examiner in an 1871 Kentucky city directory. (His son-in-law, known as Col. Breckinridge for wartime

American railroad scene illustration by Currier & Ives (1874). Library of Congress.

service in the Confederate Army, was an important lawyer. In 1875, Breckinridge already was a partner in a law firm and elected to the City Council.)

The event that more likely drove Mary and her mother into careers as working women was yet another family tragedy—the death of Dr. Desha.

It happened unexpectedly on Saturday morning, July 27, 1878, while he was going about his business as a physician. He went to the train depot at the Donerail Station near Georgetown, Ky., to await the arrival of a south-bound Cincinnati Southern Railroad passenger train to Lexington, located seven miles away. While standing on the platform, he stepped off just in time for the rapid arrival of a north-bound train.

"He was not quite quick enough in crossing the train and was struck by the locomotive and hurled under its wheels. He was left a shapeless horrible mass.

Donerail station (above). Train tracks at Georgetown (below). University of Kentucky.

The south-bound passenger train brought the news to this city, where it spread like wildfire, until everybody was anxious to hear more of the particulars," noted *The Owensboro Examiner* (Ky.) newspaper on Aug. 8, 1878.

Two years later, both Mary and her mother were listed as schoolteachers in the 1880 Census and living in her sister Issa's household, which consisted of Issa's rising political star husband Col. Breckinridge and their five offspring ranging from age 18 to 5 years old.

Col. Breckinridge at that time was referred to as one of Kentucky's foremost orators with the gift of a silver tongue. He was preparing to seek higher elected office in Washington, D.C. A few years from then, Col. Breckinridge found his name and reputation tarnished—with Mary raising a hand against him.

Col. William C.P. (known as W.C.P.) Breckinridge (1864). Library of Congress.

After the death of her father, Mary was no longer listed by her girlhood name of Molly. She had become Mary the single, working woman. It has been noted in the past that Mary and her mother became professional teachers after instructing local children. It seems likely that Col. Breckinridge— through his Kentucky blueblood connections and individual prosperity—in some way assisted with Mary's college education. Yet, he didn't entirely financially support either his widowed mother-in-law (who went from being a housewife to a working teacher at age 60) or Mary when he could

Kentucky sought to improve its public
school system when Mary taught in
the state. Public school students from
*"History of Higher Education in Kentucky."*

have. Mary's professional biography listed her as
attending the Agricultural and Mechanical College
of Kentucky (later the University of Kentucky) and
teaching in Lexington until 1885. The college didn't
allow female enrollment until legislation in 1880 that
enabled 43 students that fall semester became the
first women admitted. There was a need in the state
for a teaching program to train women teachers.

Mary could have experienced her first series of
struggles to succeed in a male-dominated career path
there. According to the university, male students
outnumbered women 5 to 1 during the 1880s.

Sometime after her mother died in 1884, Mary

left Lexington. It was said that Col. Breckinridge used political connections to secure a job for her as a government clerk in Washington, D.C. There she joined thousands of other working women struggling to survive. It is interesting to note that after leaving Kentucky, Mary constantly moved to different jobs and lived in different places. The reasons for this remain unknown, but this instability surely was difficult.

City directories show her often on the move. She appears in 1887 as a clerk in the Patent Office at one address. A year later she is a clerk in the Education Office at a different address. Then Mary moved during 1888 to teach school in Alaska. According to a DAR magazine article in 1966, Mary was one of the first American women to teach in a government position in Alaska. "There she found

U. S. Patent Office (circa 1885) where Mary worked. Library of Congress.

the conditions such that her protest caused a Governmental investigation, and she returned from Alaska to resume her work in Washington."

While living in Alaska, she maintained her close relationship with Issa, often writing letters to her sister about trying to live within a tight budget. Within a year, Mary had enough and returned to Washington, D.C., where she became a clerk at her third government agency—the Pension Office—where she worked for five years.

Old Pension Office Building (circa 1911) where Mary worked. It was decorated inside (below) in 1889 for the inauguration of President Benjamin Harrison. Library of Congress.

"Her consuming energy and abounding vitality prompted her to participate in every movement which appealed to her sense of justice; her power of initiative and executive capacity put her in the very forefront of those who crystallized into concrete form patriotic sentiments, strongest always in those who have known the hardships and been familiar with the sacrifice of war," the DAR article noted.

The Cairo was built in 1894 in Dupont Circle. It had 12 floors, which made it the district's first residential skyscraper. Library of Congress.

While at the Pension Office, Mary lived in a different location each year: L St. N.W., North Capitol, 3rd St. N.E., F St. N.E., F St. N.W., and 21st St. N.W. until she moved to The Cairo apartments (where she lived in 1897, 1899 and again in 1902) with a couple of different b o a r d i n g - house moves to Q St. N.W. in between. For a woman highly esteemed for her exceptional organizational skills and steadfast adherence to *"Robert's Rules of Order"* in civic governance, it is a

Mary Desha (circa 1894). Library of Congress.

wonder how she could keep her job and take on so many important volunteering roles in addition to such frequent moving. Perhaps her work life was her home life or she had unknown financial struggles that necessitated such erratic living arrangements.

Those who knew her described Mary as completely devoted to working for the DAR after she became a cofounder in 1890. Mary Smith Lockwood remembered Mary Desha.

"She worked hard, and if there is any picture in my mind, it is of Mary Desha, with an armful of papers in her hand that pertained to the Daughters of the American Revolution. She never walked the street that she did not have something that would pertain to our work, and that was helping it along." Mary Smith Lockwood remarked that working for DAR was more difficult in its early years since there were so few people to help. "...Mary Desha was indefatigable. Her heart was in this Society. I think she loved it most of anything in this world she was connected with."

When Mary learned that SAR voted to exclude women members, she was aghast at the discrimination. Letitia Green Stevenson recalled Mary's words,

Gen. Anthony Wayne was given the nickname "Mad Anthony" by his troops due to his fiery temper. Wikimedia Commons.

"My grandmother was the granddaughter of Col. John Montgomery, a colonel in the Revolutionary Army, and my grandfather, Gen. Joseph Desha, of Kentucky, was the grandson of Joseph Wheeler, who served with Braddock as a lieutenant, and was afterwards a solider in the Revolution. My grandfather was Mad Anthony Wayne in the

Northwestern campaign and commanded the left wing of Gen. [William Henry] Harrison's army at the Battle of the Thames. So you see I come of good old fighting stock, and it has made my blood boil whenever I have seen the 'button' worn by the 'Sons' and felt I was left out because I happened to be a woman."

Mary's contributions to DAR were numerous. For her talents, energy and perseverance, she was unanimously chosen to be recording secretary when DAR was established. She is credited with suggesting the DAR seal and also signed the national society's incorporation papers in 1891. She was given National Number 4 and became a member of what is now the Col. John Washington-Katherine Montgomery Chapter in Washington, D.C.

"Her unusual talent for organization and her business clarity of vision, combined with a rather whimsical viewpoint...all challenged my admiration, and caused me to look up to her with the respect of a younger woman, for what we called in those days 'superior qualities,'" Janet Richard reminisced many years later. "I shall always think of her as the mainspring of our early days, to whose untiring services our [DAR] Society perhaps owes more than to any other one of our early members."

Mary performed with dedication and excellence. All the while, her living arrangements remained unstable until the last few years of her life. She left

The Daughters of the American Revolution at Continental Congress in 1908. Library of Congress.

the Pension Office in 1899 to become a copyist clerk in the Indian Office. It wasn't until she moved in 1904 to The Mendota apartments at 902 F St. N.W. at age 54 that she remained living in one place. This part of her life was hidden from her numerous public

Young women in Washington, D.C. (circa 1896). Library of Congress.

achievements.

Even with all her attention and activities in DAR, Mary found time to work on other causes. In 1893, she was an active officer working alongside lawyer/ women's rights advocate Ellen Spencer Mussey in The Business Woman's Club, whose objectives were to provide like-minded women with social and professional contacts.

Mary also was a strong supporter of equal pay for women. During a February 1895 meeting of the National Council of Women, she reiterated her view that women should receive equal pay for equal work committed by men. "She held that there was no longer any question as to whether woman should or should not enter the world of business. She is there already

Hall of Representatives, U.S. Capitol. (1908).
U.S. House of Representatives History, Art & Archives.

and there to stay," noted a *Washington Post* article that discussed Mary's address. It said Mary described being an eight-year government employee and experiencing women who constantly had to perform the same work as men without any consideration for equal pay.

While Mary kept busy at work and involved in her various organizations, she had the support of her sister Issa (a fixture of Washington, D.C., society as the spouse of her prominent husband Col. Breckinridge, who represented Kentuckians in 1885 in the U.S. House of Representatives). As the last two living members of their immediate family, the sisters maintained a close relationship. Issa ensured that four of her five children bore the family name Desha, with the youngest named Mary Curry Desha Breckinridge.

Like Mary, Issa had boundless energy for causes, particularly supporting her husband—editing his speeches and attending his addresses. Issa "assisted him in all his heavy work and took the greatest care and pride in his public life," said *Lexington Herald Leader* in 1892. Called one of "the most popular ladies in Washington," Issa was also known for being "a frequent visitor at the Capitol, and never missed an opportunity to her hear brilliant husband speak," noted the *Owensboro Messenger* (Ky.) that year.

Both sisters were known for beauty and intelligence. "Mrs. Breckinridge is still very beautiful, and, as Miss Desha, was at the time of her marriage the celebrated beauty of the state," noted the *Evening Star* (Washington, D.C.) on July 29, 1883. However, Issa had a weaker physical constitution and was described as being in delicate health.

Given their similarities and close ties it must have been a huge blow to Mary when Issa died in Washington, D.C., at age 49 in July 1892 from a stomach ailment. Death was not unexpected given her delicate constitution, the *Lexington Herald Leader* noted, adding that she "was a sweet and amiable woman, and the constant companion and helpmate of her husband." Her body—accompanied by her son, Col. Breckinridge and Mary—was taken to Lexington for burial.

Tributes poured out after Issa's death, with much sympathy extended to the family and Col. Breckinridge. When he married Issa it was written that she was "one of Lexington's prettiest belles and debutantes, her father being a prominent physician, widely known" throughout Kentucky. She had been popular girl and at age 14 won a contest in 1857 for baking the best loaf of wheat bread. "In wifely devotion as well as filial, Col. Breckinridge has been singularly rich. The sparkle and glow always came into Mrs. Breckinridge's beautiful brown eyes as she sat at the feet of her husband and drank in the silver flood of his eloquence itself. Just after a speech that Col. Breckinridge made in the court house where she had sat absorbed with her soul in her eyes, she turned to a friend with a look on her face almost of rapture and exclaimed, 'He was inspired,'" recalled the *Lexington Herald-Leader* in July 1892.

At her widely attended funeral, a resolution of respect was read. It was noted she had been president of the Womans' Auxiliary Association. "Her unobtrusive and untarnished life gave added beauty to the name of woman… A sympathetic heart, an open hand, an ever ready smile was hers toward the world—her charity was broad enough to bless the human race." The sorrow described was widespread and many expressed great sympathy to widower Col. Breckinridge, who was "naturally visibly affected as the words were pronounced that bade an earthly farewell to her who had so long been the helpmate and friend."

However, barely a year later, Mary's grief at her sister's passing gave way to fury at Col. Breckinridge when he became infamous for a lawsuit brought against him. He stood accused by a long-time mistress named Madeline Pollard of failing to marry her after Issa's death. Mary—like members of the general public—first learned during the scandalous trial that Col. Breckinridge had been cheating on her sister with Madeline (the secret lover) for eight years before Issa's death.

The affair began in 1884 after Madeline, age 17, met "Willie" on a train while traveling from her school to visit an ill sister in Kentucky. Together they had three children (who all died). Then, 27-year-old Madeline sued him in court for $50,000 in a breach of promise in failing to marry her as he promised in May 1893. Instead, the "silver-tonged statesman" married his wealthy widowed cousin, who was so upset to learn of Madeline that she fell ill and was unable to leave her home. To make matters more shocking to

MADELINE V. POLLARD WHEN A SCHOOL GIRL.

Photo from *"The Celebrated Trial, Madeline Pollard vs. Breckinridge, the Most Noted Breach of Promise Suit in the History of Court Records,"* (1894).

society back then, Col. Breckinridge never denied his sexual relationship with Madeline nor their illegitimate offspring—he merely refuted the claim of a marriage proposal.

CONGRESSMAN W.C. BRECKENRIDGE, of Kentucky, is to marry Mrs. Scott-Wing, of Louisville, widow of the ex-minister to Peru, in August. He was recently reported engaged to Miss Madeline Pollard.

*Buffalo Co. Beacon* (Neb.), July 28, 1893.

Madeline and a witness testified that he wanted to wait for about a year after Issa's death to honor her memory before remarrying.

An advertisement of their engagement even appeared in a newspaper. Salacious details blazed across headlines throughout the United States and newspapers carried illustrations of portraits so readers could see what people involved looked like.

## MADELINE HYSTERICAL

Scandal Lovers on Hand

*He and Madge Were Engaged*

Mrs. Blackburn Tells How They Acted
in Her Presence

*Madeline Gives the Colonel
a Look of Hatred and Contempt*

"There was enough of sensation and scandal in the trial of Madeline Pollard's breach-of-promise suit against Congressman Breckinridge of Kentucky, to-day, to satiate even the most expectant in the fashionably arrayed masculine audience which crowded

Congressman/Col. William Campbell Preston (W.C.P.) Breckinridge (1894). Library of Congress.

the Circuit Court. Witnesses well known to all Washingtonians detailed the secret history of the life traveled by the snowy-bearded Congressman and the attractive young woman, who, seated only an arm's length apart, were magnets for the curiosity which always surrounds the personages of such a case. Except the half dozen connected with the case, there were no women in the court, but long lines of men, like the crowds before the box office of a theater, waited outside for the doors to open. These men seemed to regard the trial altogether in the light of a theatrical entertainment, apparently unconscious of the fact that there was an element of human tragedy about the affair," described the *Indianapolis Journal*, March 10, 1894.

Madeline Pollard (circa 1894). Library of Congress.

Interest was so great in the trial that Madeline's attorneys received letters from nearly every state in the Union.

Given the salaciousness of the trial and glare of the public eye, some may have expected Mary to withdraw from public, grieve for her betrayed sister and perhaps wonder how well she really knew her brother-in-law with whom she had even lived with. Not feisty Mary. She would not remain silent. She appeared at the trial as one of Madeline's first

Drawn by Chandler, of Washington.

**THE POLLARD-BRECKINRIDGE CASE—SCENES IN COURT.**

THE celebrated case of the day is the breach of promise suit, for $50,000 damages, brought by Miss Madeline Pollard against Col. W. C. P. Breckinridge, the Kentucky Congressman. Miss Pollard made the acquaintance of Colonel Breckinridge in a railroad car near Lexington, in April, 1884. She was then being educated at the expense of a certain Mr. Rodes, whom she had promised either to marry after her education was finished, or to repay him with interest the amount he had paid for her schooling. Mr. Rodes tried to compel Miss Pollard to marry him, and she, not wishing to do so, appealed to Colonel Breckinridge for advice. This resulted in an intimacy between Miss Pollard and the Colonel, whom the plaintiff claimed promised to marry her. The Congressman, however, had already been secretly married, in New York, to Mrs. Louise R. S. Wing. Sister "Cecilia," whose portait appears in the above illustration, is one of the Sisters attached to a seminary at which Miss Pollard received part of her education.

*The Illustrated American,* March 31, 1894.

witnesses. This shocking development ensured her name was carried in news reports throughout the nation in opposition to Col. Breckinridge.

"The second witness was a lady handsomely attired in green and black silk, Miss Mary Desha, the sister," noted *The Baltimore Sun,* who mistakenly referred to Issa as the first wife. In fact, she was Col. Breckinridge's second wife. His first marriage to Lucretia Clay lasted only two years because she died at age 21 during childbirth. He waited two years before wedding Issa.

Mary Desha. Public domain.

In the courtroom all eyes turned on Mary, who revealed she first met Madeline in Kentucky during the summer of 1889, but never saw her with Col. Breckinridge. Then Mary "identified a work basket as one she had given her dead sister many years ago. The latter used it continually and carried it with her wherever she went," *The Washington Post* stated March 10, 1894. The basket even bore Issa's handwriting. Whatever the evidence of the basket was to prove or how it came into the hands of Madeline's attorney remains unknown. When Mary was asked by Madeline's attorney about Issa's marriage, Col. Breckinridge waved his hand. "No cross-examination for her," he said. With that, Mary left the witness stand. Even though she presented no oral testimony against him, her presence supporting Madeline spoke volumes and cast a shadow over the congressman. It took the jury only one hour and 28 minutes of deliberation before returning a verdict— guilty, with a $15,000 fine.

Even though he lost the case and received less of a fine than Madeline expected, Col. Breckinridge boasted, according to a news account, that his Kentucky friends were "standing by him." This display of bravado didn't amount to much— Mary saw to that.

Jeremiah Morrow Wilson was Madeline's lead attorney. He had represented Indiana in Congress from 1871–74. Library of Congress.

News reports instead discussed how Madeline's lead attorney Jeremiah (Jero) Morrow Wilson received a beautiful stand of La France and American Beauty roses tied with pretty colored ribbon in a floral tribute from Mary and 27 other women. They thanked him in a note in the name of American women for taking a stance against Col. Breckinridge.

American Beauty rose (top) and La France rose (lower). Public domain.

"No flowers from Mary Desha were found in the parlors of Colonel Breckinridge," declared the *Chicago Inter Ocean* newspaper April 16, 1894. To ensure her point was made, she attached her personal card to the floral arrangement of roses with the name of Mary Desha to attract attention. Another card on the flowers came from Louise Lowell, who had testified that during her work as a government stenographer she was forced to type, under dictation, Col. Breckinridge's love letters to Madeline.

79

So moved was Wilson by the recognition given to him from Mary and the other women, that he issued this response. After thanking the women, he said "looking back over a long professional career, soon to close, there is nothing in it all that will be more gratifying to me than to have it said, if it can be said, that I have contributed to the advancement of woman and the establishment of a moral and social code that will visit upon the offending man the same measure of condemnation that it visits upon the offending woman." He said he believed the public also approved of the verdict.

Mary wrote a letter April 17, 1894 to *The Washington Post* to underscore her stance alongside Madeline in the trial. "We do not believe in making the penalty any less for the 'fallen woman,' but we do insist that the 'fallen man' shall share it—that a society that ostracizes the one shall ostracize the other." While not condoning Madeline's role in the affair, Mary opposed a double standard in the treatment of men and women.

"It is an open secret in Washington that there are women, beautiful, brilliant and fascinating, whose relations with congressmen, or other public men high in the councils of the nation, are either perfectly understood or suspected, who are met at every turn at the most fashionable functions, often in the receiving line, or, elegantly dressed, presiding in the tea-room or acting as assistant hostesses," commented the *Alexandria Gazette* on April 16, 1894, in reference to the trial. "Society knows all this, but so powerful has been the influence of the names back of them, that no one has had the courage to drop the woman or rebuke the men."

If anyone thought that Mary had washed her hands of Col. Breckinridge, they were mistaken. It was not for nothing that the DAR called her "a forceful and emphatic speaker" who "inherited the intellectual power and marked personality of her ancestors."

She issued a battle cry against Col. Breckinridge that reverberated throughout Kentucky and other Southern states when he sought reelection to Congress. With the strong support of his devoted wife Issa, he had won every election in Kentucky to the U.S. House of Representatives from 1885 through 1895 (serving in the 49th to 53rd sessions). He planned to return again to reclaim his place in Congress.

A glimpse of an unrepentant Col. Breckinridge's amid the scandal can be seen in a Louisville, Ky., dispatch to the *Chicago Tribune* after the trial. It was titled "*Breckinridge's Vanity.*" It noted that his relatives and those of his new wife had sympathy for Madeline, while blaming him completely for his downfall. "It is the general opinion that he was led on by his inordinate vanity, which made him believe he could hypnotize the court and jury with his eloquence, and afterwards repeat the experiment on his constituents. He and his wife both said as much to friends. No one now believes that Breckinridge can be nominated, or that, if nominated, he could be elected, but it is feared that he will not recognize his own defeat until he has plunged into a campaign in which he will drag out all of the scandals that are almost notorious about some of his Democratic opponents. This is understood to be the meaning of his declaration for an aggressive campaign."

Mary and other women waged a war against his bid to return to the nation's halls of power. In August 1894, she appealed directly to Col. Breckinridge's political base in Kentucky. She issued a lengthy letter, some of which is shown below: *"To the Men and Women of the Bluegrass."*

## Miss Desha's Appeal

## Col. Breckinridge's Successor Should Be a Man of Pure and Noble Character

*"I have hesitated for many days before writing this letter, because I know the prejudices of Kentucky men, and their opinion that if a woman lifts her voice against 'the established order of iniquity' she is out of her sphere. But the occasion is so grave that I venture, even at the risk of shocking my friends, to tell you some truths which it is*

*necessary for you to know, knowing well you will never hear them from Kentucky men who have been in Washington. They are bound to keep silence, either from the feeling of loyalty, which is much stronger in man than woman, for from 'a fellow feeling that makes them wondrous kind.'*

"That Col. Breckinridge will be returned to Congress has never for one moment entered my mind. The very thought of it is an insult to the state whose boast has been that her 'men were brave and her women virtuous.'

"The plain truth is that of all the immoral delegations in Congress, that of Kentucky has the reputation of being the worst....See to it, if you must have alliteration on your banners, that instead of 'Breckinridge and Brains' you have a name that will go well with morality.

*"To the women of the Bluegrass I give my grateful thanks that they have remembered my sister—her faithful, beautiful life—and have shown by every means in their power their appreciation of it, and their detestation of the man who dishonored her while living, who has desecrated her memory and disgraced her children.*

"With pride in Kentucky's past, with shame and confusion that even one man is left within her borders who is willing to see her humiliated, with an abiding trust in the final triumph of law and order, decency and morality in her midst, I am

MARY DESHA,
*A citizen of the Ashland District of Kentucky"*

Needless to say, her letter was electrifying and became "the talk of the town." Other women heeded the call to oppose Col. Breckinridge. Issa had been active in women's groups and also was a DAR member like her sister.

In Tennessee, where the Deshas had relatives, the *Knoxville Sentinel* in January 1895 ran an account of one such episode of rage, titled:

## WOMEN STIRRED UP.

"Never before in the history of Memphis have the society women been stirred up as they are over the boycott" of Col. Breckinridge, who as congressman was slated to give a lecture. When his talk was announced, the Women's Council—representing 4,000 women in 30 social and church organizations—adopted resolutions calling for women to boycott his lecture. However, some of his male and female friends were undeterred in their support for him and planned that a palatial residence would be the site to hold for him a magnificent reception. "When this move on the part of the colonel's friends was announced, it made the boycotters furious, and notwithstanding the fact that today was Sunday and a blizzard was raging, the leading lights in the Woman's Council kept the telephone busy with consultations over the wires to devise a way to make the boycott more effective."

Then the DAR, "whose members are composed of the crème de la crème of society," entered the fray. It issued the following statement.

*"In the name of the last Mrs. Issa Desha Breckinridge, a charter member of our society, and a deeply wronged woman, we appeal to all Daughters of the American Revolution do discountenance in any degree or form any courtesy or attention extended to W.C.P. Breckinridge, her husband, thereby upholding the dignity, honor and purity of our society and American womanhood."*

Mildred Spottswood Mathes in *"Souvenir of the Tennessee Centennial,"* (1897).

*Mildred Spotswood Mathes,* State Regent
*Minnie Walter Myers,* Regent of the Dolley Madison Chapter
*Jean Roberts Anderson,* Regent of the Memphis Watauga Chapter

Col. Breckinridge could not withstand such force. He lost the election, and his political career was forever spoiled. He resumed his former occupation in Lexington as an attorney, trying to remain relevant on the political scene by writing local editorials. He died in 1904.

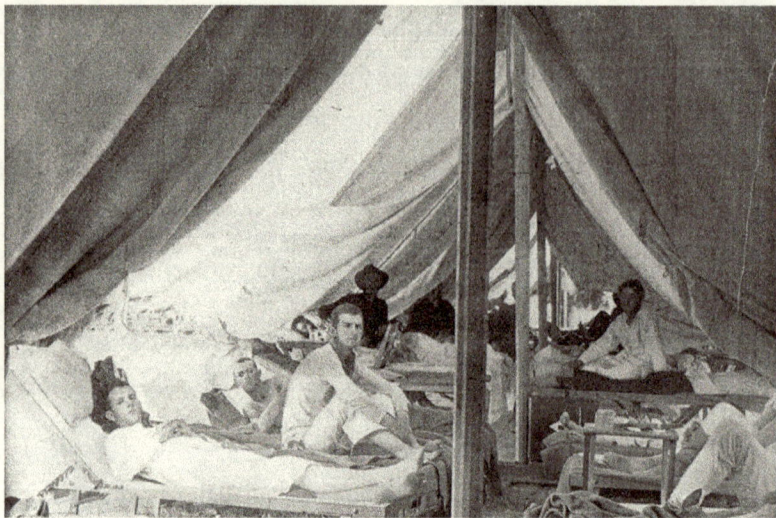

Fever wards at the Army division hospital in Jacksonville, Fla. (1898). Florida State Archives.

Meanwhile, Mary rolled up her sleeves to continue with her service projects. With the United States becoming involved in the Spanish-American War (waged over 10 weeks in 1898), Mary played a vital role. She served as assistant director of the DAR Hospital Corps. Every day after her government work, Mary worked for the Hospital Service. The Spanish-American war was the first in which military hospitals fully accepted nurses from a quasi-military unit. None died from combat, but 153 perished from diseases such as yellow fever.

"There was an enormous amount of clerical work in connection with the applications from women who wanted to act as nurses, and appropriate forms and blanks had to be sent to each applicant. Besides participating in this task, Miss Desha took charge of supplying a dozen white aprons to each nurse sent to the army," DAR noted.

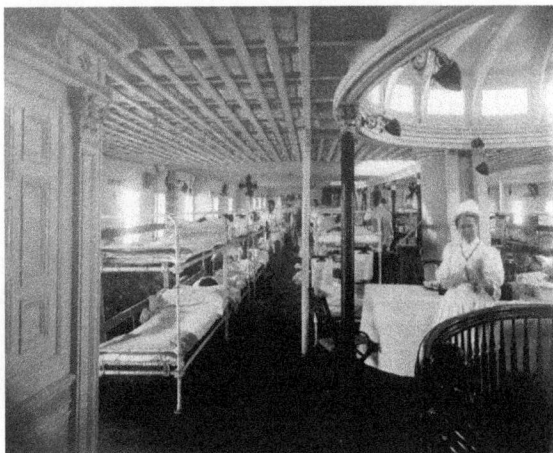

Spanish-American War: Above, Ward 3 showing bunks, patients, staff and a nurse inside a hospital ship the *U.S.S. Relief.* Below: nurses. U.S. National Library of Medicine.

"She never missed a day at the Hospital Corps room, and there she remained every night until midnight, during one of Washington's hottest summers."

One DAR member who worked with Mary at the

Hospital Corps recalled them getting an urgent request from the War Department for 50 nurses.

*The Washington Post,* Sept. 4, 1898.

Mary filled the request, which involved her walking alone at 2 a.m. to the Telegraph Office to relay the information and walking home afterwards.

The next year, Mary was instrumental in contacting DAR chapters to raise funds for the Spanish-American War Nurses Memorial, dedicated in 1905 at Arlington National Cemetery. "Nurses in the Spanish-American War worked 14-hour shifts with 20-minute lunch breaks. They provided their own uniforms, which they had to launder and maintain. Duties included dressing wounds, administering medicine, giving ice baths, preparing and serving food, and attempting to maintain sanitary conditions in tents, fields and overcrowded buildings. Many

Memorial to nurses who died in the Spanish-American War at Arlington Cemetery, Va. Library of Congress.

locations experienced nurse shortages, and some nurses worked until they were too ill to continue. The pay was $30 per month plus railroad fare to the assigned location, meals and sometimes lodging," according to Arlington National Cemetery.

Bartholdi Fountain is frozen in Washington, D.C. (1901). Library of Congress.

Never one to shy away from a cause, Mary once had enough with one of her neighbors during a chilly spring in 1905.

## COMPLAINS OF BAD SIDEWALKS

### Miss Desha Enters Charge Against Virginia Lieutenant Governor

Listing her address as 902 F. St. N.W., she asked District of Columbia commissioners to force Lt. Gov. Joseph Edward Willard (1865–1924) to remove snow and ice from the sidewalk facing his property at 20th St. and Wyoming Ave. N.W. Noting that the sidewalk hadn't been cleared since the first snowfall Nov. 13, 1904, Mary complained: "We have slipped and slided, and now we have to wade."

He replied that he was in compliance with the law, which didn't require the removal of snow, but mandated that icy surfaces be covered with ashes. However, District officials moved to issue a notification of the complaint to Willard. But Mary was not finished. While she still had the Commissioners' attention, she asked them to improve the drinking water for government employees in the District.

A year later, she was busy on another project in one of her contributions to society that is largely unknown. Mary led an effort to have a statue of Pocahontas made and placed in Jamestown. She was instrumental in the 1906 incorporation of the

Ætatis suæ 21. A. 1616.

Matoaks als Rebecka daughter to the mighty Prince Powhatan Emperour of Attanoughkomouck als Virginia converted and baptized in the Christian faith, and Wife to the wor.h M.r Tho: Rolff.

Painting of Pocahontas. National Portrait Gallery.

Pocahontas Memorial Association, of which she was recording secretary. It had 80 men and women whose goal was to collect money to build a memorial to Pocahontas, the Indian princess credited with saving the first permanent American settlement of English settlers in Jamestown. Committees were established far and wide. They wanted to commemorate the 300th anniversary of Pocahontas and the founding of the first permanent English Colony in Jamestown. Some members were descendants of Pocahontas and others were relatives of Colonial Virginians. The organization enlisted a prominent New York sculptor named William Ordway Partridge (1861–1930). He worked methodically on this important project, using sketches drawn in 1608 from the Smithsonian. For his models, he chose descendants of the Algonquins, using Native girls as models. The statue stands today as a one

William Ordway Partridge from *"The Coming Age,"* Vol. 3, No. 4, (April 1900).

of the most famous images of Jamestown Island.

Her interest in Pocahontas might have arisen in part due to Mary's work in the Indian Office. Another volunteer project regarding the famous Native American woman occurred in 1908 when Mary gave a lecture on Pocahontas for the blind at the Library of Congress.

Amid all her many activities, Mary made the DAR the centerpiece of her life's work and called it "her child," recalled Della Graeme Smallwood, DAR state regent for the District of Columbia, in 1911. "Last winter, during a protracted illness, when

Pocahontas statue (by Partridge ) at Historic Jamestowne, the location of the 1607 James Fort, near Jamestown, Va. Library of Congress.

she was alone so much in her room, she could always be found poring over records, letters, magazines, condensing our Society's past, and planning its future. She was not content to live in the twilight of memories, but in the broad light of present action and future worth," Della recalled. "In her desire to attain what she believed to be right, she did not forget justice and duty, but paid as ready tribute to those whom she opposed, as she gave disapproval to those with whom she affiliated. Hers was not the small or colorless nature that thinks of victory or defeat in any work she assumed, but she acted the present bravely and faced the future fearlessly."

DAR activities were on Mary's mind during the last hours of her life. She had telephoned cofounder Mary Smith Lockwood. They had worked together on DAR for 20 years. "She called me up on the phone, making arrangements for this great meeting we are going through now, and always had something on

Miss Mary Desha.

Photo of Mary Desha in DAR's *American Spirit Magazine* (1911).

her heart and soul that one would want to talk about," Lockwood remembered. "...we settled several things, and she said she would come around and take dinner with me the next night and see if she had got them [the planned activities] all right." An hour later the telephone rang with the news that 65-year-old Mary Desha died alone on the street while walking outside the Mendota apartments where she lived. Her body was found in front of the Beacon apartments at Calvert Street and Adams Hill Road. The cause of death was listed as apoplexy (a hemorrhage or stroke).

After her death, DAR met in Continental Hall to pass a resolution to remember the life of Mary Desha while noting with grateful appreciation her "valuable assistance faithfully given to the society since the days of its first inception." On Jan. 31, her body lay in state in Continental Hall with palms on each side of the casket.

On the day of Mary's funeral, all offices of DAR were ordered to close. The American flag at Continental Hall was flown at half-mast until the funeral ended. "Miss Desha's chair, draped with crepe, stood alone on the platform. The dear old flag which she so devotedly loved was wrapped about it, and upon it rested a large and exquisite cross of choice white flowers" from DAR. Later that afternoon a service was held there. The Marine band played as people remembered her life. It was the only funeral ever held in Continental Hall. Afterwards Mary's remains were taken to the train station for the journey to her final resting place in Kentucky. There, Mary was given one of Lexington's most imposing funerals as a cofounder of DAR and the granddaughter of Kentucky Gov. Desha.

Lexington Cemetery. Library of Congress.

Members of the DAR's Bryan Station Chapter in Lexington met Mary's remains at the train station as it arrived for burial. Funeral services were held at First Presbyterian church, the same place as Issa's funeral. She was buried in Lexington Cemetery where her parents and Issa had also been laid to rest.

Painting of Ellen Hardin Walworth by Edith Harrison Loop (1911). It cost $215 to complete and was presented to the national society by the Saratoga chapter of N.Y., of which Ellen was a member. The artist was known for her portraits. Her parents were both noted painters: Henry Augustus Loop and Jennette Harrison Loop. Image courtesy of DAR.

# Chapter 3: Ellen Hardin Walworth

Ellen Hardin Walworth dedicated her life to increasing women's rights, preserving history and supporting the U.S. military—overcoming spousal violence and a notorious family murder trial spotlighted in newspapers nationwide.

"She bore her honors gracefully, and her inheritance of courage enabled her to carry the full cup of her sorrows with a steady hand, a dignity, and a patience that crowned her more nobly than the roses of her youth and happiness," noted Ella Loraine Dorsey, in a 1915 DAR magazine article on Ellen.

Raised in a loving family environment surrounded by classical literature, politics and affluence, Ellen had inner resilience and keen intellect that helped her not only cope with adversity, but rise above many hardships that came her way.

She was born Oct. 20, 1832 in Jacksonville, Ill., as the eldest child of Col. John Jay Hardin and Sarah Ellen Smith Hardin. She came into this world the year following her parents' marriage. Her siblings were:

- Martin Davis Hardin (1837–1923),
- Lemuel Smith Hardin (1840–1916), and
- Elizabeth Hardin (1844–1848).

Both her parents maintained equally strong ties to their new home in Illinois and birthplaces in Kentucky. Her maternal grandfather Horace Smith was an early settler of Mercer County, Ky., (named after a

Revolutionary War general).

The Hardins were an illustrious family. A cousin Benjamin (Ben) Hardin (1784–1852) was a Kentucky attorney who served five terms in the U.S. House of Representatives. In addition, the family was related (as cousins) to Mary Todd of Lexington, Ky., who would marry Abraham Lincoln. It has been stated that Lincoln

Benjamin Hardin, Public domain.

met his future wife in Ellen's home at a social event hosted by her father and mother.

Her great-grandfather Col. John Hardin (1753–1782) served in the Revolutionary War and was sent in 1792 by Gen. James Wilkinson, commander at Fort Washington, on a peace mission to hostile Native Americans. Col. Hardin had been chosen due to his courage and qualifications. However Col. Hardin had premonitions about his fate in the dangerous mission. His last letter to his wife stated: "But oh, my dear love, as I write and meditate on myself, to think I have left a peaceful, safe, plentiful, and so dear a family, and thrown my life into the hands of a cruel and savage enemy, I cannot prevent the tears from flowing of my eyes at present." Soon afterwards, while traveling with his interpreter and a group of Natives, he was shot to death in an ambush by a group of Native Americans while traveling under a flag of truce. He had been born in Fauquier County, Va., and had served as an officer with the Kentucky militia in a fight with Miami Indians in 1790. Hardin County, Ohio is named after him.

Ellen's grandfather Martin D. Hardin (1780–1823) was a powerhouse. In his career of public service, he was a distinguished politician, lawyer, a former Kentucky Secretary of State and Speaker of the House, U.S. senator, and former

Portrait of Martin D. Hardin, Ellen's grandfather. Public domain.

officer in the War of 1812. Her father John Jay (John J.) Hardin was also a man of notable achievements. His parents' eldest son, he was 13 years old when his father died. Despite his young age, John J. successfully

managed his father's estate in the Blue Grass region of Kentucky near the city of Frankfort. He was known for his classical education, sharp intelligence, eloquent speech and strong ambition. Despite having important family

Ellen's father John Jay Hardin, Public domain.

connections in Kentucky and starting his law career there after graduating from Transylvania University, he relocated to Illinois at age 21 to make a name for himself. He returned to Kentucky briefly to marry in 1831 and brought his bride Sarah back to Illinois, where he built her the first brick house in Jacksonville. From this homestead, his career flourished as he operated a large farm and raised a family.

John J. became a mustering officer in the Illinois Militia during the Black Hawk War (1831–1832) and was in Capt. Abraham Lincoln's Company of Mounted Volunteers. Both Lincoln and John J. became friends and political rivals. John J. is credited with possibly saving Lincoln's life by rushing to an island where Lincoln was preparing to fight a duel with Gen. James Shields. Lincoln had written a letter published in a newspaper mocking

Young John J. Hardin. Color engraving: Abraham Lincoln Presidential Library & Museum.

Shields, who demanded satisfaction. Just as Lincoln chose a cavalry sword as his weapon (despite the fact that Shields was an expert shot), Harden stopped the duel and brokered resolution. In 1832, John J. was appointed State's Attorney for Morgan County. His political career flourished first in the state House of Representatives where he served from 1836–1842. Next he went to the U.S. House of Representatives in the 28th Congress, representing the Whig party from 1843 to 1845.

Young Ellen (Nelly) Hardin. The Saratoga Springs History Museum.

Called by her nickname Nelly, Ellen was raised with care regarding her education. She grew up on the family farm in the country with cattle, horses and hunting dogs. At the age of five, her father put her on a horse in one of the great pastures and began to teach her to ride by saying, "Now, my daughter, do not let him throw you off." She grew up with notable visitors such as Lincoln and other politicians frequenting the family home. She attended Jacksonville Academy as part of her formal education.

Ellen was only 14 years old when Congress declared war on Mexico in May 1846. A call was made for 50,000 volunteer soldiers. These were mostly chosen from western and southern states closer to Mexico (thus making troop transports less costly) and whose men had better firearms skills than those in northern industrial cities. Illinois was to provide three regiments of infantry or riflemen from its disorganized militia. Ten days after the governor asked for 30 companies of volunteers (who could elect their own officers and company) to serve for a year, 75 companies wanted to join. The First Regiment was organized with Ellen's father commissioned as its colonel. Col. John J. Hardin and his regiment mustered into service in July 1846, leaving for New Orleans in the journey to Mexico.

At age 37, Col. John J. was killed in Mexico while leading the final charge during the Battle of Buena Vista in February 1847. "On that fatal day in which he lost his life, he was conspicuous at the head of his command, waving his

Death of Col. John J. Hardin by N. Currier (1847). Library of Congress.

men on to the charge and his voice was heard ringing clear and loud above the clash of arms and the storm of battle, cheering on to victory. His regiment repulsed the enemy several times with great slaughter," noted *The Ottawa Free Trader* (Ill.) newspaper on Aug. 6, 1847. Despite suffering from a leg wound, he "succeeded in firing his pistol, and a Mexican fell under the shot, but another bullet pierced him in the neck, and five lance wounds were found in his body," wrote Helen, in a December 1879 article called the *"Battle of Buena Vista"* in the *Magazine of American History.* It contained her own account of her father's death.

Abraham Lincoln played a leading role in a John J. Hardin Memorial Meeting regarding the Battle of Buena Vista on April 5, 1847 in which he proposed a motion and read aloud a public gesture expressing "sympathy and regret" at the deaths of John J. and "his companions in arms from Illinois, who nobly fell in defense of their country's honor," as Lincoln paid tribute to their bravery.

His body was recovered and sent for burial to his family in Jacksonville. A few months later, the Hardin family braced itself for the funeral service. "It was a grand and imposing scene. The immense concourse—the character and standing of the mourners—evinced the deep sympathy and respect entertained for the memory of the beloved Harden," stated *The Ottawa Free Trader* on July 23, 1847. "Illinois be proud of so noble and gallant a son." The moving funeral scene was recalled 100 years later in the *Journal of the Illinois State Historical Society* in June 1947 as a "mournful pageant." The funeral procession consisted of a long line of carriages and horsemen processing along the road amid bell tolls and cannon fire. All businesses were closed in respect as an atmosphere of sorrow spread. "Immediately behind the hearse bearing the coffin, followed the noble war horse of Hardin, led by a trusty servant, who had followed him with unwavering fidelity and attachment, through all his varied and

> ### Proceedings of the John J. Hardin Memorial Meeting regarding the Battle of Buena Vista, 5 April 1847
>
> IN MEMORY OF THE GALLANT DEAD.
>
> On Monday last there was a large meeting of our citizens held at the Court House, at which the following proceedings took place:
>
> Pursuant to previous notice, a large and respectable meeting of citizens of Springfield was held at the court house, on Monday afternoon, the 5th inst., for the purpose of taking into consideration the propriety of adopting measures to co-operate with citizens in other counties of this State, in their expression of sympathy and regret for Gen. J. J. Hardin and his companions in arms from Illinois, who nobly fell in defence of their country's honor, and to pay a suitable tribute of respect and admiration for the bravery and fortitude of our volunteers at the battle of Buena Vista, in Mexico.
>
> On motion of Hon. A. Lincoln,
>
> Judge Treat was called to the chair, and on motion of J. T. Stuart, Esq.,[*Esquire*] Thomas Moffett, Esq. and S. S. Brooks were appointed Secretaries.
>
> The Hon. Mr. Lincoln then explained the objects of the meeting in a few appropriate remarks, when he offered the following resolutions, which were unanimously adopted:
>
> *Resolved:* That, while we sincerely rejoice at the signal triumph of the American arms at Buena Vista, and contemplate with the highest pride, the imperishable honor won by our Illinois brethren, upon that bloody field, it is with the deepest grief we have learned of the fall of the many brave and generous spirits there, and especially, of that of Col.[*Colonel*] J. J. Hardin.
>
> *Resolved:* That William Pope, Mason Brayman, John Calhoun, Antrim Campbell and Geo. L. Huntington be a committee to correspond with the people, or committees of other counties, and especially with Col. Hardin's immediate neighbors at Jacksonville, on the subject embraced in these resolutions; and that said committee have power to fill vacancies, and to call subsequent meetings, when, in their judgment it becomes proper.
>
> *Resolved:* That the proceedings of this meeting be published in both the papers in this city.[1]
>
> On motion adjourned.
>
> SAMUEL H. TREAT, Chn'n.[*Chairman*]
>
> THOS MOFFETT,
>
> S. S. BROOKS, Sec's.[*Secretaries*]
>
> [1] While the Sangamo Journal published the proceedings, the other paper in the Springfield, the Illinois State Register, did not publish them.

Proceedings of the John J. Hardin Memorial Meeting regarding the Battle of Buena Vista, April 5, 1847. Abraham Lincoln Presidential Library & Museum.

perilous career upon a foreign soil. To us this was the most touching feature in all the scene of that day. It seemed to bring the subject right home to every heart, and realize to us, as nothing else did or could have done, the sad certainty of our loss. There, right before our eyes, saddled, bridled and caparisoned, was the noble animal upon which the bold Hardin had ridden from many a weary mile, over many a desert and dangerous waste. …The sight was truly impressive and melancholy."

Undoubtedly, the Hardin family was devastated by this loss. Ellen, as the eldest, had enjoyed a close relationship with her father. Before John J. left for Mexico, "Abraham Lincoln promised that, if his friend did not return, he would act as a foster father to his son Martin D. Hardin, then 10 years old," according to Cecile A. DeBirny, in a DAR article in 1965. Lincoln fulfilled this promise with Martin, who would have a distinguished career as a West Point graduate and Union officer in the Civil War.

At age 36, Ellen's mother Sarah Ellen Hardin found herself a widow with three children. The youngest was Lem, age seven. A U.S. Census for 1850 shows Sarah lived in Kentucky with her three children (Ellen then 18 years old) and owned real estate valued at $30,000. The family soon found themselves in the midst of an elite East Coast social circle after Sarah married another widower named Chancellor Reuben Hyde Walworth, age 63, of Saratoga Springs, N.Y. on April 16, 1851 in Kentucky.

Chancellor Reuben Hyde Walworth. Painting by Nelson Cook (1808–92).

The marriage took place at the home of famous Kentuckian Dr. Christopher Columbus Graham, noted pioneer, intellectual and veteran. The marriage to Chancellor Walworth gave Sarah and her children a boost in status due to his national influence, high society connections and East

105

Coast prestige. This alliance would have a profoundly negative impact on Ellen's life.

Sarah and her three children moved to Walworth's mansion called Pine Grove, named for its location amid a grove of majestic trees where outdoor swings hung from lofty branches. The estate was located on the corner of Broadway and Vandam streets. The wooded area next to the mansion was used as a public grounds for entertaining and leisure.

"In personal appearance, the Chancellor was not distinguished. He was a small lean man, and in his latter days had long iron-gray hair and beard, and looked rather haggard. His face was intellectual, and his eye was keen," noted *The Albany Law Journal* in 1876. Apparently, he also had a noteworthy athletic ability and achieved fame in his youth for jumping.

Side view of Walworth Mansion Pine Grove. New York Heritage Digital Collections.

Even at the age of 47, he "astonished" another judge and others in a social gathering by leaping over parlor chairs and challenging others to compete with him. Walworth also liked riding horses. "It was his habit early in the evening to play cards, chess, or backgammon with his family and his guests, and then to study and work at night, often until 3 or 4 o'clock. He was a good storyteller [with] hearty laughter. In his simple and spacious house at Saratoga, he exercised a generous hospitality, seeking and receiving the distinguished persons who resorted to its famous spa," the *Law Journal* stated.

Ellen Hardin age 16. The Saratoga Springs History Museum.

Sarah's new husband had other similarities with John J. Hardin. Both were outgoing and enjoyed active social lives. They also were self-made men, intellectuals, lawyers, military veterans, and politicians who served in Congress. Other shared characteristics included their ambition and pride in family heritage.

Chancellor Walworth's mansion contained a Walworth coat of arms because he claimed lineage with Sir William Walworth (who died in 1385) the Lord Mayor of London. Chancellor Walworth was born in Connecticut and raised in New York. His father fought with Continental Army during the Revolutionary War. At 12 years old he was so determined to get an education that "he went from home and worked through the winter, mornings and evenings, for his board, that he might have

Illustration of Saratoga Springs, N.Y. (1876). Library of Congress.

the advantage of a better common school than that in the vicinity of his father's residence," noted an 1852 magazine article on distinguished Americans. "At the age of 16, he himself was a teacher of a village school during the winter months. He was also engaged in the same employment during the following winter." He continued as a farmhand until an accident with an overturned wagon loaded with wheat injured his ankle, preventing him from continuing farming and nearly crippling him. He began to work as a country store clerk until he met a lawyer. Despite a humble education in a common school while working the family farm, Chancellor Walworth decided to study law at age 17 in a law office of a prominent attorney in Troy, N.Y. He was admitted to the bar in 1809 and became a county judge in 1811. However, his legal career was interrupted by the War of 1812; he served as aide-de-camp to Maj. Gen. Benjamin Mooers. He briefly branched out into politics and was elected to the 17th Congress (1821–1823). That foray into politics was his last before he made his mark as a jurist. After leaving Congress, he became a judge for five years in the 4th District of New York, moving to Saratoga Springs in 1828. Then he was appointed to be the prestigious Chancellor of New York.

"Brought up a farmer till the age of 17, deprived of all the advantages of a classical education, and with a very limited knowledge of chancery law, I find myself, at the age of 38, suddenly and unexpectedly placed at the head of the judiciary of the state; a situation which heretofore has been filled by the most able and experience members of the profession," Walworth said, in an address to the Bar when he was promoted to Chancellor. He served with distinction, giving legal opinions, and was in demand for settling disputes until a new state constitution abolished the court in 1848. Known as always ready to help widows and orphans with legal troubles, he also had a widespread reputation of disapproving drinking alcohol.

Another similarity between Ellen's mother Sarah and her new husband Walworth was they both lost their spouses in 1847. His first wife Maria Ketchum Averill Walworth died at Pine Grove in April 1847. They married six months before the War

109

of 1812 began and had six children:

- Mary Elizabeth (1812–1875),
- Sarah Simonds (1815–1874),
- Ann Eliza (1817–1895),
- Clarence Augustus Walworth (1820–1900),
- Mansfield Tracy Walworth (1830–1873), and
- Frances (1834–1839).

The Chancellor's first wife Maria Ketchum Averill Walworth. She was the mother's of Ellen's husband. Painting by Nelson Cook.

When Ellen and her family joined the Chancellor's household none of his children were living there. His three daughters were married—Mary Elizabeth to Edgar Jenkins, Sarah Simonds to John M. Davison and Ann Eliza to Rev. Jonathan Trumbull Backus—and raising families of their own. Due to the Chancellor's age difference

Mansfield Tracy Walworth. The New York Public Library.

with his second wife Sarah, most of his daughters were already wed around the time Ellen was born.

His strictness in requiring that correct legal

110

procedures be followed in his courtroom was viewed negatively by his peers. "One of his official faults was the habit of enforcing the rules of his court with illiberal exactness, sometimes with acrimony, especially in cases presented by young or inexperienced lawyers. This gave him the ill will of that class of the profession," remarked Lucien Brock Proctor in his 1882 book called *"Lawyer and Client—or, The Trials and Triumphs of the Bar: Illustrated by Scenes in the Court-room, Etc."* It also earned him an unflattering nickname. "As he always wrote his name with some ostentation, 'R. Hyde Walworth,' certain members of the junior bar, taking advantage of this, in retaliation for sharp raps received from him, gave him the name of 'Raw Hide Walworth.'"

Clarence Walworth from *"Life Sketches of Father Walworth: with Notes and Letters,"* by Ellen's daughter Ellen H. Walworth (1907).

The Chancellor apparently had high, but doomed expectations that his two sons would follow in his legal footsteps. His eldest son Clarence had tried to be like his father by becoming a lawyer in Rochester, N.Y. in 1842, but soon gave it up in favor of religious life. He left his law practice to attend an Episcopal seminary for three years. "My father's personal library of law books, a large and fine collection, was sent home to him forthwith, and when I parted with these very little of law

111

remained with me," he recalled later. His religious journey did not end. In 1845, despite strong family opposition, he converted to the Roman Catholic faith and become a priest. (Father Clarence would become an important figure in Ellen's life.)

The youngest son and surviving child was Mansfield (Manse) Tracy Walworth—who had graduated in 1849 in law studies from Union College in Schenectady, N.Y., during a time when his father served as its trustee. He was among only 13 people in his graduating class that year.

Manse had a reputation within the family as a troublemaker who lacked discipline and disappointed his father—in contrast to his serious-minded elder brother Clarence, who sought a profession to be of service to others. Apparently the Chancellor had tried to carefully guide Manse's education into a law career.

An interesting and unflattering description of Manse is given in the 1882 book *"Lawyer and Client"* by Lucien B. Proctor, then a law student who went to the Chancellor's home in Saratoga Springs to take an oath of office and sign to be admitted to practice law. Unlike with other courts, the Chancellor's courtroom was held in his mansion. The law student asked directions of a young man, who turned out to be Manse. "His form, set off by a fashionable dress, was exceedingly graceful and attractive; but it was not his form and dress that chiefly attracted attention; it was the bold, buoyant, intelligent expression that presided over his handsome face. There was something in the restless though penetrating and

Young men on a porch in Saratoga Springs, N.Y. (circa 1865). Library of Congress.

semi-impudent glance of his eye that indicated a haughty, arrogant nature, and an ill-regulated mind." The two had a brief conversation in which Manse apparently behaved rudely and spoke sarcastically.

It is unclear when Ellen first met Manse, a handsome young man with blue eyes, dark brown flowing hair and a high forehead. She was 18 years old when her mother married the Chancellor in April 1851. According to personal correspondence, Ellen had fallen in love with her step-brother by December of that year. Manse was described as brilliant and dashing, and Ellen a beautiful blonde. The following year would bring both sorrow and joy to the family.

In February 1852, Ellen joined Manse in converting to Catholicism. They were influenced by Father Clarence, who returned from Europe where he was ordained with great enthusiasm for his new Catholic faith. She embraced this new religion, going against the wishes of her mother and brother Martin D. Hardin. The Chancellor and Sarah welcomed their baby Reuben Jr. in April 1852. This joyous event was followed by a lavish society wedding. Ellen and Manse were married in July, a few months after he received his law degree from Harvard University.

Father Clarence performed the marriage ceremony at the Church of St. Peter in Saratoga Springs.

"Long before the hour announced for the ceremony, the hotels began to pour forth crowds of visitors eager to witness a ceremony so novel to most of them as a Catholic wedding, and when the bridal party arrived at the church every nook and corner was preoccupied and it was with difficulty they succeeded in reaching the places reserved for them. The beauty and fashion of the Springs were present and hundreds were unwillingly forced to relinquish all chance of access and to return back to their almost deserted hotels," noted the *New York Herald*. The elite were in great attendance. The Chancellor's family friends included James Fenimore Cooper and Ralph Waldo Emerson. The best man at the wedding was Washington Irving. The bridal party was outfitted in the height of fashionable attire for the wealthy. "The bride and her maids were richly [clothed] in white, with exquisite wreaths of the choicest and most lovely flowers about their foreheads, and long and delicately wrought veils, and immense

Spring in Saratoga Springs (1867). The New York Public Library.

114

America's literary giants at Ellen's wedding: Washington Irving of Sleepy Hollow fame (left, 1860). James Fenimore Cooper (1860), author of *"The Last of the Mohicans."* Poet Ralph Waldo Emerson (1875). National Portrait Gallery.

trains of white satin. The groom and groomsmen were dressed with great discrimination, and in the most approved wedding gear."

After the ceremony, the bridal party was transported from the church in carriages to Pine Grove, where the Chancellor hosted a spectacular wedding reception. Over 100 guests were in attendance. "It was a beautiful sight; the brilliantly lighted rooms and flitting figures of the great, with whom the room was fairly swarming," the *New York Herald* noted. A sumptuous dinner was served and guests enjoyed the festivities (which started with the 10 a.m. wedding) until their departure just before midnight. "Young and old joined in hearty wishes for the prosperity and happiness of the married couple."

Sorrow, violence, tragedy and public notoriety

Ellen Hardin Walworth.
By Nelson Cook.

would befall this couple. Manse would forever be known as a wife beater—who bit Ellen's fingers to the bone in a rage and penned vile letters to her in blood, including written threats wrapped around gunpowder and bullets.

The Walworth family experienced a great loss with the death of the Chancellor's beloved six-month-old son in October 1852. Sarah's sons Martin D. and Lem, and the newlyweds Ellen and Manse all continued living at Pine Grove, which the Chancellor expanded to 55 rooms and a courtyard.

"The [Chancellor's] second marriage was, like the first, a very happy one. The new wife brought with her to Pine Grove not only a sweet and loving temper, but a certain Southern style of hospitality which consorted admirably with her husband's own disposition. A cheerful circle of friends soon gathered around her. She loved to keep open house, and many more familiar faces passed in and out than ever thought to ring the bell, or wait in the parlors," noted William Leete Stone Jr. in *"Reminiscences of Saratoga and Ballston"* (1875).

Other notable guests to Pine Grove included former U.S. presidents Martin Van Buren and Millard Filmore as well as past N.Y. governors DeWitt Clinton and

William L. Marcy. The Walworths and Hardin children remained close to and visited with Abraham Lincoln and Mary Todd Lincoln. From all outward appearances, life was good at the Chancellor's home with his beautiful young wife, Lem and the young newlyweds.

From Pine Grove, Manse began his career as an attorney, while Lem, age 19, was a law student. Martin D. Hardin had left for West Point in 1854, graduating in the Class of 1859.

Manse and Ellen started a family of their own in Saratoga. Together, they had eight children, three of whom died young: John at age seven in 1862, Mary Elizabeth (Bessie) at 20 months old in 1858, and

Pine Grove, the Chancellor's Mansion, from *Harper's New Monthly Magazine* (Aug. 1876).

Sarah Margaret at seven months in 1872. None of their children would ever achieve as much fame as their first child Francis (Frank) Hardin (born in 1853). This son would cause a nationwide scandal, bring untold grief to Ellen and forever smear the Walworth name for fatally shooting his father Manse in a hotel room. The other children were:

- Ellen Hardin (Nellie) Walworth born in 1858,
- Clara Teresa Walworth born in 1859,
- Mansfield Tracy Walworth Jr. (who went by

his middle name) born in June 19 1861, and

• Reubena (Ruby) Hyde Walworth born in 1867 in Louisville, Ky.

*Ellen's Troubled Marriage*

Mansfield Tracy Walworth Jr. and Reubena (Ruby) Hyde Walworth. By Nelson Cook.

Tensions began to grow in Pine Grove. Manse found being an attorney boring. He took to alcohol and became increasingly violent. According to one of his cousins, Manse "was, at all times, a man of violent passions, and when under the influence of liquor was at times absolutely brutal. He, on many occasions, assaulted his wife, and even threatened to make way with her. Friends on many occasions interfered and endeavored, for the sake of the wife and children, to preserve peace, but without avail. Whenever he was under the influence of liquor, he was uncontrollable, and his wife and children were the first to feel his resentment."

Manse turned his career aspirations to becoming an author. His first book, published in 1853, was a nonfiction work called *"The Mission of Death, a Tale of the New York Penal Laws."* It dealt with discrimination against Catholics in New York and the hanging in 1741 of John Ury, believed to be a Roman Catholic priest and who was executed. Despite this achievement, Manse wasn't ready to completely stop practicing law. In February 1855, he was among three New York attorneys admitted to practice law in the U.S. Supreme Court in Washington, D.C.

In the meantime, Ellen occupied her time as a society wife and mother. In August 1860, her name appeared among the best dressed women at a Saratoga Springs grand opening ball of the season at the Union Hotel. She "wore a graceful and becoming robe of pink" while in the company of the ladies who "were generally dressed with exceeding taste and elegance," noted the *New York Herald*.

To all outward appearances, Ellen and Manse were a happy couple, but their marriage began to fray after only a few years—with arguments between the two and violent outbursts from Manse. "He was unfitted for marital life, and proved that fact by treating his wife badly, and by subjecting her to causeless whims very soon after the marriage," wrote *The New York Times* after Manse's death.

In 1861, Ellen, age 26, took her children, including infant Mansfield Tracy Jr.,. and moved away from

Grand Union Hotel in Saratoga Springs (1860). Library of Congress.

Saratoga Springs with her brother Lem to a farm about three miles from Louisville, Ky. She left behind Manse, the Chancellor and her mother in favor of relocating to Kentucky where her relatives lived. It was a drastic and difficult move. Helen left the North for the Southern states during a heated time as the Civil War became a reality. Starting in January 1861, pro-slavery states began seceding from the Union; war came with the Battle of Fort Sumter in April 1861. Although Kentucky, a border state, declared neutrality in the conflict, its citizens were split in their loyalties. She bought an old estate worth $30,000 near Louisville, Ky., called "Bird's Nest," where she occupied herself with farming vegetables and raising her young children. (Lem had been a law student in N.Y., and it is likely he continued his education in Louisville since he practiced law there at the end of the Civil War.)

One newspaper description of their unhappy marital life declared later "it would seem that every possible indignity and insult were heaped upon Mrs. Walworth, by the man she married. Their married life, from the few first happy years, was a continual quarrel, not on her part, but on his. Her children were treated by him, not as father should treat his children, and she was regarded by her husband not as a man should respect and love his wife. From unhappiness their marital quarrels verged into absolute enmity, and Walworth frequently struck her."

Louisville, Ky., (1876). Library of Congress.

During this first separation, Manse was supposed to join her in Kentucky but instead went to Washington, D.C. He later declared himself to be a citizen of Louisville with a wife, children and property there even though he had never been to see his family at the farm. Apparently, Ellen used inheritance money from her father to buy the farm to live with her children and Lem. She didn't meet up with Manse again until they were reunited for a week during a visit to Saratoga in 1863. While Ellen and the children tried to survive in Kentucky after the Civil War was declared, Manse had a close call with the law in Washington, D.C.

Instead of joining the military to fight on either side of the war, Manse found himself a job at the State Department and became involved in a Confederate spy ring with a woman of intrigue (known as Mrs. Morris). The pair was arrested Feb. 7, 1862 at 4 a.m. in her room in Brown's Hotel—on the order of Maj. Gen. George B. McClellan. Even though he was from New York, Manse was sympathetic to the Confederate cause. His cousin John L. Barbour said he witnessed Manse once dressed in a Confederate uniform and that Manse lied

BROWN'S MARBLE HOTEL,
BETWEEN 6th & 7th STREETS,
Pennsylvania Avenue, Washington City.
T. P. & M. BROWN, Proprietors.

Brown's Hotel where Manse was arrested. Photo by Mathew Brady. Washington, D. C. Public Library.

to him about being an officer in the Rebel army.

News of Manse's arrest spread like wildfire throughout the country due to his father's prominence. In discussing the arrest, the Buffalo, N.Y., *Commercial Advertiser* declared: "The Chancellor has two sons—Clarence, the elder, and Mansfield, the younger. The former is a Catholic priest, and is well known in this city—the latter is a sort of nothing; a wild, reckless, impetuous, daredevil fellow, without much principle or reputation… For his father's sake, we trust that young Walworth may be able to prove his innocence. There are many who love and respect the father, though they must … denounce the son."

A Feb. 19, 1862 article in *The New York Times*, "Young Walworth," told of his downfall. "The War Department has proofs which is considered conclusive, that young WALWORTH is a spy for the rebels. His relations with the fascinating widow MORRIS have been peculiarly intimate. In his trunk were found pistols, powder, and a bowie knife." Manse had been employed by the State Department.

Federal authorities were unaware at that time that Mrs. Mason, who pretended to be from France, was really Ada Hewitt from Alexandria, Va. When she appeared in newspaper accounts

Mrs Morris in Washington, D.C. Photo by Mathew Brady. The Wilson Library, University of North Carolina at Chapel Hill.

a decade later, it was written: "Of her powers of fascination there can be no question, statesmen and warriors having surrendered at discretion to her charms of form and intellect," noted *The Alexandria Gazette* in April 1872. "Years have passed lightly over her head, and the hand of time has touched gently the features that in earlier days marked her as one of the most beautiful of nature's daughters. She is of medium height, black hair, and eyes of sparkling depth and blackness, rich brunette complexion, figure slightly inclined to embonpoint, and strikingly attractive, and possessing great piquancy of manner and self-possession."

According to the federal government, Mrs. Augusta Heath Morris (also known as Miss Ada M. Hewitt and Mrs. Mason) was a spy on a mission to collect information to pass along to the enemy. She was connected to another espionage agent William T. Smithson, a banker, in a large Confederate spy ring organized by Lt. Col. Edward Porter Alexander, who was stationed at Confederate winter quarters at Centreville, Va. As well as thought to be masterminding the spy ring, Alexander was the head of the Confederate signal corps. At the time of the arrests, Centerville was of strategic importance to both sides as a supply depot because of its proximity to roads. (Nearby is Manassas where the Battles of Bull Run were fought.)

Lt. Col. Edward Porter Alexander (1866). Public domain.

Mrs. Morris was accused of corresponding with another spy Thomas John Rayford (whose real name was Brig. Gen. Thomas Jordan, a Confederate spy ring operative), who misled detectives by dating his letters as if he was in New York City when he was elsewhere. The alluring Mrs. Morris also socialized with a dozen men, including Union Army officers and other Southern-sympathizing women. Several newspapers wrote about her being taken into custody.

## ARREST OF A FEMALE SECESSIONIST

"A lady, calling herself Mrs. Morris, who came here [Washington, D.C.] from Richmond sometime since alleging that she had been compelled to leave on account of expressions of sympathy with the North, was arrested today and locked up in

Brig. Gen. Thomas Jordan (1861–65). Library of Congress.

the Capitol Hill Prison. She is charged with giving information to the enemy regarding the position and strength of the Federal troops and fortifications in and about Washington. Mr. Walworth, son of Chancellor Walworth, of New York, clerk in the Adjutant-General's Office, has also been arrested and imprisoned on charge of acting in complicity with her. This Mrs. Morris, who is a gay, dashing and sprightly widow, it will be remembered offered for $100,000 to explain the Confederate Army signals. This offer was not accepted but for prudential reasons it was deemed advisable to keep a strict watch upon her and the result has been her arrest, which took place at 4 o'clock this morning while she was in bed at her hotel."

—*The New York Herald*

Manse's incarceration for espionage was shocking. It is easy to imagine the scandal this created for his esteemed father Chancellor Walworth, not to mention his wife and Harden in-laws—relatives of Abraham Lincoln's wife. His brother-in-law Martin Davis Hardin was a Union Army colonel serving in the 12th Pennsylvania Infantry and a West Point graduate.

Public suspicion fell on his wife Ellen living in Kentucky with their five children, one of whom (John Jay Walworth) died there at some time during 1862 at the age of seven.

Was she a Rebel and plotting against the Union? The whispering must have been a source of concern for her, especially since many of her father's military friends were fighting against the Confederates.

Next offering his services as a spy for the Union, Manse wrote to Maj. Gen. John C.

Martin Davis Hardin became a Union general during the Civil War. He is shown after losing his arm in the fight. Library of Congress.

Fremont at some point before June 27, 1862 when Fremont was relieved of his command at his request by the War Department. (Fremont was upset at having to report to an officer of a lower rank.) In his note, Manse offered to provide information from the South on the Nashville road near Mammoth

Cave, Ky., "by the medium of my wife" and on another topic with information from a woman in Danville, Ky. "I have made important discoveries concerning the attack on Washington which my duty requires me to carry to Washington at once."

Traveling on Echo River in Mammoth Cave (1893). Library of Congress.

There is no evidence of Ellen's support for either side in the conflict. Her mother, Sarah, however, demonstrated loyalty to the Union as well as to Manse.

Sarah Walworth was criticized after she published a card giving her version about why her stepson and son-in-law Manse had been wrongly arrested. She "had the bad taste to claim that her son having inherited Democratic views from his father, is not the victim of prosecution for political opinion's sake" given that Abraham Lincoln was elected president on the Republican ticket, remarked the *Daily Cleveland Herald* on Feb. 19, 1862. It quoted her card: "He [Manse] has said and done no more than thousands of Democrats who are now filling the ranks of the Federal army, and enjoying the highest employments of Government offices. If he has been arrested, it is from the determined rancor and misrepresentation of enemies here, which some few indiscretions on his part have made for him." Her justification of

Old Capitol Military Prison during the Civil War on 1st St. and A St. N.E. in Washington, D.C. It is now the site of the U.S. Supreme Court. National Archives and Records Administration.

Manse's behavior did him no good, but demonstrated how the Walworth family attempted to cover up his deeds.

Manse was made a prisoner in the old Capitol Military Prison. He was brought before a federal military commission on March 31, 1862 composed of Edward Pierrepont (an attorney appointed by President Lincoln to try cases of state prisoners in federal military custody), Gen. John Adams Dix, and Erastus D. Webber, secretary.

During his stint in prison, Manse apparently witnessed the murder of a fellow Confederate prisoner and friend Lt. Jesse B. Wharton of Hagerstown, Md., fatally shot by a guard form the 91st Pennsylvania regiment after leaning out a window and refusing to move back inside. The victim and guard had exchanged angry words before the incident. There was a dispute about whether the shooting was provoked or not. Manse, always one to espouse his thoughts, sent a card with his version of events to a New York newspaper, which was republished June 11, 1862 in a pro-Southern Ohio newspaper called *The Crisis*.

## EXPLANATION OF THE CONFEDERATE SHOT AT WASHINGTON CITY.

### CARD FROM M. T. WALWORTH.

*Editors of the Atlas & Argus, Albany:*

*"My attention has been called to an article in your paper relating to Lieut. Wharton, who was shot by a sentinel in the Old Capitol Prison, Washington. I have no question in my mind that the same spirit of fairness which characterized your paper before I became a citizen of Kentucky, still prevails, and will induce you to give this article a place in your columns. I speak from knowledge of the occurrence. I was arrested by order of Gen. McClellan, imprisoned for nearly three months in the Confederate prison, and am still a prisoner with the parole of Saratoga county, and am obliged to report to this Government daily my whereabouts. I was beside Lieut. Wharton in the room when he was shot, heard the altercation with the sentinel, and the charges made by the dying man. I was his friend, and when the fellow prisoners left him with his wife he requested me to remain with him and her until he died.*

*"He did not provoke the altercation. He was resting with his arms upon the windowsill, and when ordered*

to take in his head, withdrew his arms and stood perfectly erect, and a few inches back from the window. The words of the sentinel, which provoked Wharton's sarcastic retort, were not the order to take in his head, but the sentinel's use of opprobrious epithets and cursing him.

"He was in no mood for quarreling, having that very moment closed a Bible, from which he was reading aloud his mother's favorite chapter, and remarking upon his respect for the Episcopalian religion, occasioned by her life. When the altercation had gone on for a few moments, and while Wharton was standing a few inches back from the window, with his left hand resting upon his right elbow, the sentinel, under the order of an unseen person below in the prison yard, raised his musket to the second story window and fired. The ball passed through his left hand, his right arm, and thence through his right breast, going entirely through him, and striking the wall beyond.

"He was my friend, and I shall vindicate his memory.

"It would be proper for those who have friends [who are] prisoners in Richmond, to make some effort to have a fair examination of this case, for retaliation upon prisoners by the hasty and uncontrolled soldiers of either side, should, for the sake of humanity, be postponed by the good sense of the belligerents.

"Lieut. Wharton had resigned from the U.S. Army in Utah, and is a nephew of a member of the Cabinet

*at Richmond. His relatives in Virginia and Maryland*
*are of the most prominent families."*
—MANSFIELD T. WALWORTH

While some people did their utmost to behave humbly and get out of prison, Manse retained his difficult and haughty behavior. His custody was transferred from the military to State Department authorities where his case was listed in its Record Book under *"Arrests for Disloyalty."* Typically, all that was required for captured Confederates to be released from imprisonment was to swear an oath of allegiance to the U.S. government and desist from supporting the Rebellion. Manse, however, earned the headline *"Stubborn"* after being held for three months in prison.

"Mansfield Walworth, a young man well known in this vicinity, and who was arrested in Washington about two months ago, charged with conveying information of importance to the rebels, is still confined in Washington. He refuses as yet to accept the condition imposed by the commissioners upon State prisoners, viz: that he shall take the oath of allegiance and return to Saratoga county, and report daily to his father, Chancellor Walworth, until further orders. He declares that he would prefer to go South and remain there until the war is over. His wishes of course will not be heeded by the government."
— *The Buffalo Commercial* (N.Y.), April 9, 1862

Soon afterwards, Manse did as the government ordered and went to Saratoga. Justice J.H. Johnson administered at the Old Capitol prison the oath of allegiance to Manse, who gave his word of honor that he would not assist the rebels in any way. Manse also was prohibited from writing letters to the South during the war. The Federals held onto Mrs. Morris until May after she agreed not to return north of the Potomac River for the rest of the war. She journeyed to Richmond and met up with Alexander, who described Mrs. Morris in a June 1862 letter to his wife. "Mrs. M., I think is not a model of virtue however patriotic she may be. I am going to give her a few hundred dollars of the Secret Service money & send her off to the South," he declared.

As the death toll mounted in the Civil War and

COMMISSION RELATING TO STATE PRISONERS,
*Washington, April 1, 1862.*

W. P. WOOD, Esq., *Superintendent, &c., Washington.*

SIR: You may release Mr. Mansfield T. Walworth upon his taking the oath of allegiance and engaging upon oath that he will leave the city of Washington forthwith and repair immediately to his paternal home in Saratoga County, N. Y., and report daily therefrom to the Hon. Reuben H. Walworth, and that he will not leave the county of Saratoga nor hold any correspondence himself nor be engaged in any with any person in the States in armed insurrection against the authority of the Government of the United States without permission from the Secretary of War.

Very respectfully, yours,

JOHN A. DIX,
EDWARDS PIERREPONT,
*Commissioners.*

*"The War of Rebellion: A Compilation of the Official Records of the Union and Confederate Armies,"* 55th Congress, House of Representatives, 1897.

sacrifices were made (with brother-in-law Martin Davis even losing an arm among his many battlefield injuries), Manse lived under his father's watch and let his imagination lead his nascent literary pursuits.

Never one to hide his feelings, Manse wrote several letters to Union Army officials while under his father's custody in New York. Being confined to live under the same roof as his imposing, no-nonsense father ensured that Manse stayed out of trouble. His father was a well-known abstinence man and president of the American Temperance Union. However, the Chancellor's conservative outlook did little to curb his son's excessive behavior.

Secretary of War Edwin M. Stanton in a Civil War photo. Library of Congress.

In April 28, 1862, Manse apologized for unflattering remarks he made against Secretary of War Edwin M. Stanton. At the same time, he acknowledged that he was forced to report his daily whereabouts and unable to leave the county of Saratoga unless released by Secretary Stanton. Manse maintained he was a citizen of Louisville—not Saratoga—in what appears to be an unsuccessful bid to move to Kentucky where Ellen and the children lived. One wonders how Manse insisted he was a citizen of Kentucky (not New York) when he had never lived there or been there once Ellen left him. It is equally baffling as to how Manse acquired Confederate sympathies when he and his parents were products of the North. His writings make derogatory comments about Yankees and yet he was one. Ellen's actions indicate she sided with the Union. Thus Manse's political views are a mystery. Government records also contain the following bizarre letter Manse wrote to Stanton.

*Hon. E.M. Stanton*

*Dear Sir,*
*"I wish to apologize for hasty expressions I have made in your regard and referred to by the Commissioners in my examination. I am sorry that my rage at being treated to imprisonment in view and for my long and zealous services should have induced me to refer to improper motives of yours. This apology is weak but sincere.*

*"I cannot shake off the confidence of the rebels, having once gained it. In my unjust imprisonment I still sought rebel confidence for my country's sake. But I suppose the same indifference which induced the government to treat lightly my offer to go to Centreville on secret service will prompt the government to slight my remark, that I have found in my imprisonment other clues to the Knights of the Golden Circle\* as*

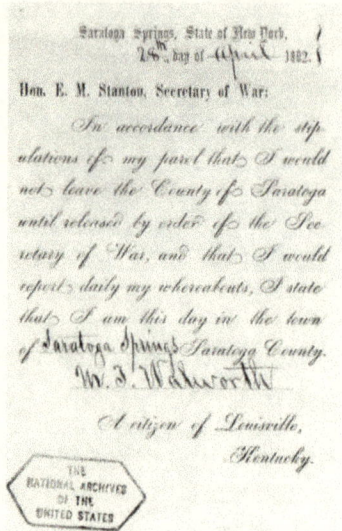

*relating to Genls [Charles Pomery] Stone and [George B.] McClellan than those I heard from Sec. Mallory in Richmond and found embodied in my information brought from the South to Sec. [William H.] Seward and Genl. [John C.] Fremont and for which it is a burning shame that I am unpaid."*
*Respectfully,*
*—M.T. Walworth*

* The Knights of the Golden Circle were a secret society for Southern nationalism from 1854-63.

In August 1862, Manse wrote to an Army office insisting he was a citizen of Louisville and asked to be exempt from being drafted in the New York Army or militia. He asked for a certificate or order of exemption. He also expressed thanks for receiving permission from the Army or militia to write to Ellen. When not sending letters to the military, Manse devoted himself to writing a fictional tale, loosely based on real people and places called *"Lulu: A Tale of the National Hotel Poisoning,"* published in 1863. It is a mystery why the book's copyright was registered in the District Court in Kentucky when Manse was living in New York. The book received favorable reviews.

• "There is a great deal of merit in 'Lulu.' It is one of the better class of sensation novels."—*New York Post*

• "Lulu may deal too freely with living well-known characters, and may have other defects, but it is a charming book." —*Brownson's Quarterly Review*

- "Hon. Wm. H. Seward's character cannot be mistaken. The Hon. Chancellor Walworth, 'the philanthropist,' the Hon. Erastus Corning, 'the Railroad king,' the Hon. Samuel Nelson, 'the Jolly Judge,' the Hon. Samuel Blatchford and John V.L. Pruyn... hundreds declare they recognize [real people] in this book, as also several ladies in high social positions." — *The Sentinel*

- "Upon the basis of that curious wholesale poisoning which took place in Washington at the time of Mr. Buchanan's inauguration, the author has built a little *roman de societie,* which is sparkling and clever. We are informed that Mr. Walworth was one of the victims of this plot and narrowly escaped with this life. As for his characters, *'Lulu'* is a most lovable woman, 'Bess Stapleton' is an accomplished flirt, and 'Harry Carter' is a presentable young man, who esteems himself happy in escaping the latter and becoming the husband of the former." — *The Philadelphia Inquirer*

Not to be outdone by his younger brother, Rev. Clarence Walworth put his hand to pen to write a book called *"The Gentle Skeptic, or Essays and Conversations of a Country Justice on the Authenticity and Truthfulness of the Old Testament Records."* Published in 1863, the book was written to defend the Bible. [Clarence's writings never achieved the acclaim as his sibling's work.] Ten years after his treatise on the Bible, Clarence wrote about the afterlife in a book called *"The Doctrine of Hell"* (1873). Another work is bettered remembered today not for its quality, but rather a scathing review written by Oscar Wilde and published in the *Pall Mall Gazette* in November 1888. The book was called *"Andiatorocte, Or The Eve of Lady Day on Lake George and other Poems, Hymns and Meditations in Verse."*

Wilde's review of the book is as follows: *"Andiatorocte* is the title of a volume of poems by the Rev. Clarence Walworth, of Albany, N.Y. It is a word borrowed from the Indians, and should, we think, be returned to them as soon as possible... The most curious poem of the book is called Scenes at the Holy Home: 'Jesus and Joseph at work! Hurra! Sight never to see again, A prentice Deity plies the saw, While the Master ploughs with the plane.' Poems of this kind were popular in the Middle Ages when the cathedrals of every Christian country served as its theaters. They are anachronisms now, and it is odd that they should come to us from the United States. In matters of this kind we should have some protection."

Irish poet/author Oscar Wilde (1882). Library of Congress.

While Clarence explored religion in his work, Manse stuck to pulp fiction based on his experiences that appeared to target bored affluent women. He penned a serialized story, *"Love for Life—A New England Story,"* in a London magazine for housewives called *The Family Friend* magazine. It appeared in four installments starting in the Midsummer 1864 edition. The love story was intertwined with characters and places from his life. A main character was a lawyer, another a U.S. Supreme Court judge in Washington, D.C. His imaginary mind created a village called Tattletown with two sets of rival factions: the "Reds" and Blues." In one of its 29 chapters called: *"The Wavering Heart,"* he wrote: *"As the spell of her beauty and the charm of her conversation at length dissipated the thin veil of restraint, his fluent tongue regained its power. Then language, with its indescribable influence, revealed to her the deep enthusiasm of his heart and his keen sense of the beautiful and romantic in life appeared to her each instant. She discovered the kindred fire which warms the meeting of two bright intellects brought into contact for the first time in the arena of taste and judgement."*

Upon his retirement, the Chancellor also decided to become an author. While Manse was letting his imagination flow in writing, his father pursued family genealogy, particularly researching his mother's Hyde family. It was all thanks to William Hyde of Norwich, who traveled from England to America in 1633; he provided the starting point for this epic ancestral ode. The Chancellor penned 1,446 pages in a two-volume book, *"Hyde Genealogy,"* published in 1864. So determined was the Chancellor to find Hyde relatives to record in his writings that he earned an amusing description in *Appletons' Journal* (July–December 1878).

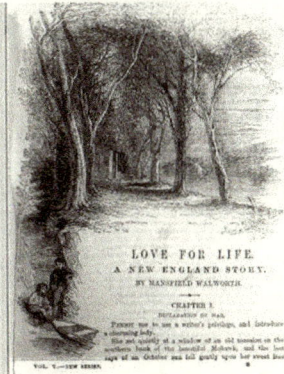

Sample pages of "Love for — A New England Story,"
in *The Family Friend* (London) magazine, 1864.

"...chancellor Reuben Hyde Walworth, as genealogical as he was genial, whose researches for his 12 ancestors among the original 35 had raised the very dust of the dead. He had become so well known for this diversion, especially his pursuit of those who held a certain family name, that the profane had been thinking of putting under his shingle, 'Cash Paid for Hydes.' When it was his turn to speak, the old graveyard uptown awoke, and then not only the 12 ancestors which centered in himself, and the general cousinship which he could claim with everybody, appeared, but it seemed as if the entire horizon awoke, too. ...From memory and memoranda the venerable spokesman of the fathers emitted a luminous cloud of family names, which shortly burst into such a prodigious shower of spray that every face in the multitude was sprinkled. Such a general christening had never been seen before." Evidently, the Chancellor was very proud of his Hyde ancestry and thought much of himself. Perhaps this arrogance explains why

Yours with esteem
R. H. Walworth

his youngest son, Manse, who he personally spent so much care raising, became so conceited and self-entitled.

Manse's troubles as a traitorous spy put no stain on the Walworth family. In fact, the Chancellor's prestige also continued to grow. Despite lacking a college education, the Chancellor was awarded honorary degrees from Yale, Princeton and Harvard. From time to time during retirement, he continued to practice law as a Chamber counsel and referee. His paternal shadow of power and influence obviously spared Manse.

Manse's next book was also a success. *"Hotspur: A Tale of the Old Dutch Manor"* was published in 1864, also with a copyright registered in Kentucky where Ellen continued to live as Manse remained in New York. The novel began: "The distant, tinkling bell of memory recalls the town of C___. The noble old State of New York boasts of no fairer garden spot within its broad limits. The elms love to adorn the streets of C___. There their graceful branches droop lower, their symmetrical trunks shoot higher, and their foliage wears in summer a more emerald luster than in any other portion of the State. Like faithful sentinels they guard the many aristocratic mansions of the wealthy, and the

DAILY CLEVELAND HERALD.

TUESDAY EVENING JULY 12, 1864.

Hotspur. A Tale of the Old Dutch Manor, by the author of "Lulu"................... 1 50

neat white cottages of the middling classes. They bear themselves as if there were proud of their character of protectors against the fierce rays of the summer sun. Noble, old trees—many a bright intellect has studied and blessed your beauty; many a lovely eye detected through your branches the silver stars of God."

The book met with acclaim in a review by the *Evening Star* newspaper. It declared the novel "exceeds in interest and general worth, any book of similar kind which of late years has beguiled our leisure. We read it en route for the country. Let every tourist possess himself of the clever work."

Manse showed no remorse nor changed his arrogant behavior. His nasty attitude toward military officials overseeing his parole is evident from other letters he wrote that year to his military minders while seeking permission to venture into New York City for a vacation and to pursue his writing career. In a letter to Maj. Gen. John Adams Dix, from New York, Manse continued to complain.

*Oct. 12, 1864*

*Dear Sir,*

*"You know personally under what circumstances I was sent to the limits of Saratoga County and promised not to leave those limits until released by order of the Secretary of War.*

*"I have been here quietly attending to the business for two years and a half having taken the oath of allegiance as required by yourself & judge Pierport.*

*"I am publishing books for two years past and convenience requires me sometimes to go to N.Y. city in furtherance of their sale. Why should I not be allowed to go to N.Y. city this winter?*

*"Will you not be kind enough to write to the Secretary of War in my behalf making such terms for my being allowed to visit N.Y. as you please. I will report to yourself there if so required daily or any other way. Father regards your influence as more likely to secure this result than any other. Why should I not be released absolutely. I have faithfully fulfilled all obligations and I have no other wish than to remain loyal. Will you not be kind enough to write and intercede for me to the Secretary of War. To their add to the feelings I cherish towards you of gratitude for your former kindness."*

*Yours very truly,*
*Mansfield. T. Walworth*

Ever the prolific writer of letters, Manse followed up shortly afterwards with a letter to the Secretary of War.

*Saratoga Springs Oct. 14th 1864*
*Hon. E. M. Stanton, Secretary of War*

*Dear Sir*
*"In accordance with the terms of my release from the Old Capitol Prison I took the Oath of Allegiance and promised to remain within the limits of Saratoga County until release by order of the Secretary of War.*

*"I have remained faithfully within the limits of this county for two years and a half.*

*"I am publishing books, one of which I send you by this mail. I intend to devote myself exclusively to writing and publishing.*

*"In furtherance of the sale of my books it would be both pleasurable and useful for me to visit New York City from time to time.*

*"Why will you not send me an order to do so, requiring me to report to Major. Genl. Dix. While in the city, if you deem that essential?"*

*I am yours very respectfully,*
*Mansfield T. Walworth*


Much to Manse's delight, he was unconditionally released from parole at the recommendation of Secretary Seward on Oct. 29, 1864. This paved the way for his public rehabilitation. He began to write for *The Home Journal* magazine of New York, which also published articles penned by his friend Washington Irving.

## *Ellen's Civil War Years: Single Mother in Kentucky*

Throughout the Civil War, Ellen maintained a low profile in Kentucky. She worked hard at the family farm to support herself and children. It is said she arose at 4 a.m. daily and gathered fruit and vegetables with her children to sell at the Louisville market during the tumultuous war years. After a battle in Virginia, hundreds of half-starved federal troops made their way to Kentucky. Two hundred camped at her farm, where she fed them with her meager provisions for days until the U.S. Army sent food. In a strange coincidence, several Army officers remembered her father since they were from Illinois and Indiana.

Ellen's mother remained in New York, while her brothers chose different sides in the Civil War. Young Lem left Ellen and her youngsters on the farm in Kentucky join the Confederate cause. Evading a blockade in January 1864, he enlisted in the Second Kentucky Cavalry as a private in the Kentucky Confederate Volunteers. He fought under Kentucky plantation owner Gen. John Hunt Morgan, known as the "Thunderbolt of the Confederacy." Lem was wounded in the leg in May 1864 at the Battle of Cove Mountain as the Confederates prevented a Union division from reaching the nearby town of Wytheville, Va., to damage a southern railway link to Richmond. For the remainder of his life, Lem suffered from a wound he sustained in that battle that never completely healed. Sent to Kentucky to recover from his injury, Lem eventually decided to abandon the Confederate cause. If his brother Martin were to find him convalescing at home with Ellen in Kentucky, Martin would have been forced to turn Lem into authorities. So Ellen helped dress Lem as a woman and flee to neutral Canada (composed of several British colonies instead of the unified country we know today), where he remained until after the war.

His injury is noted in a letter his mother Sarah wrote to her family friend President Lincoln. In Dec. 19, 1864, she pleaded with Lincoln on behalf of her son and mentioned his deceased father who had been friends with Lincoln. While it remains unknown if President Lincoln took any action regarding the matter, her letter is preserved among the Abraham Lincoln Papers at the Library of Congress. It is also interesting to note she addressed her letter to Mr. rather than President and she signed it only with her initials. This would seem to demonstrate a familiarity rather then being formal.

*Mr. Lincoln,*

*"I have a young son Lemuel S. Hardin, who has been a short time in the Southern Army, [and] has been severely wounded. He has made his way through the lines and is now in Canada. He is crippled for life and is anxious to return to his home and family. He has been a resident for the last three years in Louisville Ky. and at a country seat near the city...*

*"If you think favorably of my petition for my son to return to his country, and to his home and*

*mother, to be a good boy in future, you can make the conditions. I can see no good reason why he should not be allowed to return home.*

*"After a young man has 'sown his wild oats', or 'seen the elephant' he is often better prepared to settle down and become a sensible man, he has a better appreciation of home and the advantage of a good position. Mr. President, I claim your indulgence [sic] in favor of my petition not on the merit of the case but as an act of clemency to a wayward youth. My waif of a son is endowed with many of the good qualities of the noble man from which he comes both of head and heart."*

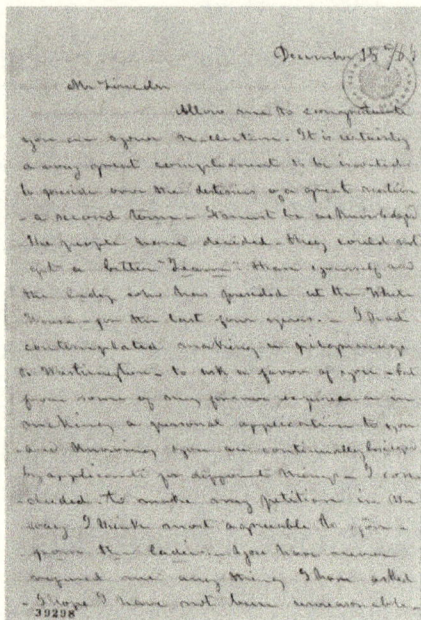

*Yours respectfully,*
*S.E. Walworth*

Nearly six months after the end of the Civil War, Lem was pardoned by Kentucky Gov. Thomas E. Bramlette on Oct. 18, 1865, the same day Lem signed an allegiance to the Constitution and the United States. [Gov. Bramlette's daughter Corinne later married Lem's nephew and Ellen's eldest son Francis (Frank) Hardin Walworth. Since the family lived in Kentucky during the Civil War, Frank was educated there in Louisville schools as a youth.]

Ellen's other brother Brig. Gen. Martin D. Hardin achieved distinction as a Union officer during the Civil War, brevetted five times for gallantry. In December 1863, then-Col. Martin commanded two regiments at Catlett's Station, Va., and was inspecting pickets near a railway line when a group of six Rebel guerillas under famed John Mosby, disguised in long Union uniform

Brig. Gen. Thomas E. Bramlette, of 3rd Kentucky Infantry during the Civil War. Library of Congress.

overcoats, attacked. Hardin was shot through the arm (the bullet breaking his bone) and his horse was killed. The injured arm—already previously disabled by a sever wound from the second battle of Bull Run—had to be amputated. (Many years later, Gen. Hardin visited the battle scene where he lost his arm and learned it had been buried on land owned by his ancestor under a colonial grant in America, according to 1924 annual report by *Association of Graduates of the U.S. Military Academy*.)

Hardin returned to duty in spring 1864 to defend the area north of the Potomac and again was wounded. He also fought at Gettysburg. Hardin retired from the Army in 1870 due to his Civil War

Brig. Gen. Martin Hardin wore a medal after the Civil War. Library of Congress.

injuries. Ellen, while close to both her brothers, remained extremely proud of her brother Gen. Martin's wartime achievements.

According to the terms of his parole, Manse was allowed the freedom to visit Ellen and the children in Kentucky for six weeks.

In 1865, Manse was offered the post of general secretary of the New York Association for the Advancement of Science and Art. However, a newspaper account in the *Evening Star* declared that Manse's doctor had advised him to wait six months before accepting the position and to delay writing his new book called *"Stormcliff: A Tale of the Highlands,"* which was published in 1866. He was already achieving fame for his books *Hotspur* and *Lulu*. In fact, according to the *Evening Star,* "His unfinished book is pronounced by the literary critics far superior to *'Hotspur,'* which is having such an extraordinary run."

## Ellen: A Battered and Abused Wife

After the Civil War, Ellen and Manse had periods of reconciliation. She tried to remain cordial despite his violent outbursts. Sometimes they lived together as a family and then separated. Manse's abusive behavior continued. One incident occurred in summer 1865 when Ellen and the children visited Saratoga. Ellen and her father-in-law had gone out for the evening with two friends at a hotel. When they returned home after 10 p.m., they found Manse had remained in his room and locked them outside. Ellen noted later that "after knocking a couple of times, he opened the door. He looked with fury at me, and with a terrible oath exclaimed, 'I will show you how you will leave me of an evening again.' He seized me by the arm and shook me with great violence. He pushed me against the furniture and literally tore the clothes from my back. When I took up my infant to leave the room, he commanded me in the most threatening manner to lay it down again and myself. In an hour or two, he fell asleep and I escaped from the room. He had been in the habit of acting in a very violent manner for a great many years."

Once when they were in the same dwelling, Manse went to her to complain about one of her brothers. She recounted that at "about 9 o'clock, after spending a quiet evening, he came to my room door, and as I opened the door I saw that he wore the same terrible expression, and, with both arms uplifted, he uttered those fearful exclamations, 'Hardin shall not rob me of my wife and children,' although we had not seen my brother for a long time previously. He then struck me violently, and raised me in his arms in the most violent manner and threw me on the bed, where I lay for some time unconscious. On another occasion he suddenly sprung on me and struck me." Manse even bit Ellen's finger through to the bone during another rage.

"Everyone at all acquainted with Mrs. Walworth, or with her friends, were aware, they said, of the continued and brutal insult daily dealt her by her husband

Younger Ellen. Public domain.

during the last 10 years of their married life," noted *The New York Times* in 1871. "Those who knew her in the days of her beauty and happiness scarcely recognized her, so changed was her appearance."

There must have been significant social pressure and financial reasons for Ellen to remain in the marriage. She stayed and had two more children with Manse. Named after her grandfather, Reubena (Ruby) Hyde was born in Louisville in February 1867. After the Chancellor died later that year in November, Manse left Ellen for a time to live in Albany with his brother. The Chancellor's death at age 79 brought out even more savage behavior in Manse—he couldn't get over the fact that his father bequeathed a greater inheritance to Ellen and the children than to himself.

The Chancellor's will was recorded in court Feb. 24, 1868 with his son Clarence and son-in-law

Presbyterian Rev. Jonathan T. Backus of Schenectady as executors. The Chancellor rewrote his will four months before his death in November 1867 in such a way that his widow Sarah inherited the bulk of his money,

Bedroom in a wealthy New York mansion (circa 1870). Library of Congress.

property and household belongings, and a trust was established for her to be administered by her children, who were also made beneficiaries. (According to the 1860 U.S. Census, the Chancellor's property in New York was valued at $20,000 and his personal estate was worth $75,000.)

Manse was totally left without any of the most valuable part of his father's inheritance. Instead, he was bequeathed a $1,000 annuity in joint support of himself, Ellen and their children. If the couple separated, Ellen was to receive half the annuity from the trust to be paid directly to support her and the children. It was said the Chancellor left no money or valuable property directly to Manse as a sign of disapproval about his past behavior and his abuse of Ellen. All that Manse alone inherited was one of four equal parts of his father's law library, the Chancellor's agate seal with the Walworth surname (already in

Manse's possession) and an enameled portfolio that belonged to Manse's deceased mother. "I declare," the Chancellor wrote, "that the cabinet purchased for him by his mother, together with the collection of minerals, shells and other curiosities in and on the same already belong to him, and are not to be inventoried as part of my property. I also give to him my *'Alisons History of Europe'* and my *'Hammonds Political History.'*" Even the piano went to Ellen, and the family coat of arms to their son Frank. All of Manse and Ellen's children received valuable books, family mementos, paintings, collectibles and photos. Manse was furious. The following letter he wrote in 1872 to Ellen provides a keen insight into his disturbed mind and long grudge regarding the disinheritance.

*Publication House of Carleton & Co.,*
*Under Fifth Avenue Hotel*
*New York, August 14*

*"Listen to these terrible words. They will show you how keenly and fiercely I feel the humiliation of Reuben H. Walworth's will, and what a Scot, the descendant of King Malcolm, will do when all has been taken from him. Reuben H. Walworth always hated me from my cradle. He always hated anyone who was high-spirited and would speak out their thoughts. He always liked cringing hypocrites, like Eliza Backus [his married sister Anna Eliza Walworth Backus] and [brother] Clarence Walworth. Although he saw*

*my ambitious spirit he hated it because it would not toady to his favorite Yankees. Hence from my cradle he persecuted me and headed me off in every pursuit or speculation. I could not please him in anything because I would not whine to him about his favorites. Everything that I ever wrung from him, even my pay in the Spike [legal] case, was wrung from his fears. The only reason that he did not omit my name from his will altogether was that he respected my talents and hoped I would write his life. He knew nobody else would. But he has stung me into madness and broken up my family by placing me in the humiliating position of being under a trustee, and that trustee my brother, who has neither ambition nor heart. From his grave he glares at me and says: 'Ha! Ha! You were always proud and high-spirited, but by my will I have put in your side a thorn for life. You have no dignity under it, and it will sting you to your grave. The only ones of my name who have any dignity under my will are your sons, Frank and Tracy, who will bear my name to posterity.' Now, Ellen Hardin, knowing that I am helpless under that will, if you will persist in trying year by year to see how much of that trust property you can get out of me by threats of law, by personal blandishments to my trustees, or by any other means; if you doubt and will not see that I out to have something for my entire life, whether he intended me to or not, then mark what will be the finale of my vengeance upon that dead scoundrel dog who has made me so pitiable before me and before you.*

Chancellor Reuben Walworth in his final years. Public domain photo.

*"I will—so help me the demons who wait upon the persecuted and the proud spirited and the revengeful—I will, when stripped by you of my property (and you mean it at last), plunge my dagger into Frank and Tracy's heart, and cut off the Walworth name forever. God damn him, he has elevated them and degraded me, and you gloat over it. I have not one single firm right under his will. This you believe, and this has been the cause of your despising and abandoning me. With cold calm purpose you contemplate my eventual beggary and humiliation. I will kill your boys and defeat the damned scoundrel in his grave and cut off his damned name forever. Now you just persecute me about that property, and keep this thorn alive in my heart, but the eternal God I will kill them and you too. Now you hunt my property any further ____ ____, and I will kill your boys as well as you. The ____ dead villain shan't rob me of wife, children and property. If I can't have anything, I'll have revenge. ____ I have lost nearly everything which makes life tolerable."*

154

After the Chancellor's death, Manse made it his life's mission to berate Ellen over the inheritance. Witnesses said he began to treat Ellen and the children with even more cruelty, especially with his father no longer around to restrain him. "He neglected his family most shamefully, failing to supply sufficient food, frequently leaving them destitute of coal, barely clothing them decently, and at all times treating them in the most coarse and brutal manner. At this time, he was receiving the entire of the annuity from his father's estate, and was earning a fair competence from his literary pursuits. He dressed himself with scrupulous nicety, and was conspicuous in his hospitality to his male friends and acquaintances at the clubs and restaurants, taking care that his own living should be not merely comfortable but elegant," reported the *Chicago Tribune*. "Thus he expended all this income on himself, to the almost total neglect of his family."

Ellen's mother stepped in to provide basic necessities for her daughter and grandchildren. Manse became more physically violent with Ellen, who "submitted meekly to the wrongs heaped upon her by her husband, taking care never to complain to others of the treatment she received" despite notable bruises and other injuries left on her body.

"At the time of his father's death, he [Manse] was subject repeatedly, perhaps every day, to those violent furies, in which he would abuse his father and brother. He did not expend all his fury on me.

155

He would strike the furniture and break it with whatever he might seize in his hand. He did this very frequently after his father's death," Ellen recalled.

In 1868, she and the children returned to the Pine Grove family home in Saratoga. Apparently, Manse had grown restless and convinced Ellen to sell the estate and give him the proceeds. The need for money appears to have been an issue that year due to a sidewalk sale in June of part of the Chancellor's library. The sale generated great interest in the public, anxious to get their hands on a relic from the old man's belongings. "The old desk from which he issued his Chancery edicts so long was one of the things that attracted most attention," declared *The New York Times*.

During this time, Manse was writing a nonfiction work on the life of N.Y. Chancellor Robert R. Livingston (1746–1813) and a fiction novel. Manse published his murder mystery called *"Warwick; or The Lost Nationalities of America"* in 1869. It met with some success despite harsh words from critics. "This is one of those books with the critics invariably feel called upon to condemn, and which the public (or rather a certain portion of it) as invariably feel called upon to read—a wild attempt by a writer with neither talent nor originality, to make industry and pedantic concerns do the work of though, careful observation and culture."—*The Eclectic Magazine of Foreign Literature, Science and Art*, August 1869. A different view was taken of the book by *Harper's*

*New Monthly Magazine* in June of that year. "It is not easy, having commenced to read the book, to lay it down unfinished. ... The heroine is a curious admixture who dances, discusses theology, rides an untamable steed in perilous places, and teaches in a mission school with equal zest and equal success." The review makes note of Manse's imagination in his unreal tale. It is interesting that he included the great Mammoth Cave of Kentucky in his plot, which was the same cave he wrote about in his offer to spy for Union troops in 1862.

"*Warwick*" enjoyed modest success. According to one estimate, it sold 30,000 copies, which would have earned Manse from $4,500 to $5,000 in royalties. But one New York journalist thought the actual amount was only half, with Manse's book sales "due to the art of purfling [ornamenting the borders]."

Unsatisfied with the fruition of his budding literary career, Manse continued to mistreat Ellen, whom he blamed for perceived affronts. His abuse of her was common knowledge among their family members, children and friends. In the summer of 1869, he became violent after his children received clothes and other presents as gifts from his sister. Ellen said later that "..without any previous signs of displeasure, he arose suddenly in the night, and swore at his sister in a most violent manner and commenced to search the house for articles and destroyed them. ... He was always extremely pale and had the look of a wild beast..."

At some time before 1869, Ellen moved with the children to Washington, D.C., where she worked as a government clerk. She had tried to find a job in New York but could not. Like many other women before her, she came to the nation's capital where respectable administrative jobs were plentiful for women struggling to make ends meet. Her eldest, Frank, attended Georgetown College. An article in the *National Republican* newspaper in April 1869 mentions a White House reception hosted by the president's wife, Julia Dent Grant. Ellen was among the guests (including senators and generals) received in the Blue Room. The women were elegantly attired. Mrs. Grant wore "a fine corn-colored moiré antique dress, with rich black lower corsage and full trains, black lace shawl, coral jewelry, hair dressed with curls, over chignon, and adorned with a crimson rose."

First Lady, Julia Dent Grant (1876). Her friendship with Ellen would be important during the Spanish-American War in 1898. Library of Congress.

Ellen's mother continued to live in Saratoga, but Manse left to live with his brother Clarence in Albany. Ellen's independence was short-lived, however, and she returned 18 months later to New York after she lost her job due to politics.

Ellen continued to stay in the marriage until

her mother Sarah couldn't stand the abuse of her daughter and grandchildren to go on any longer. The couple had been staying with her mother in New York City. Likely Sarah feared for Ellen's life after Manse assaulted his wife in 1870 while she was in the latter stages of pregnancy with Sarah Margaret.

"Not only had she been beaten until the black and blue spots were everywhere visible, but her hands had been bitten by the brutal husband, his teeth tearing the flesh away until the bones were laid bare," the *Chicago Tribune* noted.

Despite her advanced age, Sarah decided to get help from Manse's blood relatives, who decided to hold a family council under the guidance of brother Clarence. The family declared Ellen must leave Manse. Her brother Gen. Martin Hardin, then stationed in Buffalo, N.Y., traveled to New York City to personally remove Ellen and the children on Jan. 26, 1871 to the home of Walworth relative John Maret Barbour, a powerful lawyer and judge of the New York City Superior Court.

Ellen finally left Manse for good. With great speed, · she sought to end the marriage. A lawyer was enlisted to draft the divorce proceedings with help from Gen. Martin, who relocated to a swank New York City hotel called Hoffman House on Broadway and 25th Street. It was there that Manse tried to prevent Ellen from terminating their marriage. One day in late January 1871, the divorce papers were hurriedly being

Original Hoffman House in *"Illustrated New York,"* (1888).

drawn up by the lawyer, Ellen and her brother Martin. Ellen had moved into the hotel briefly to stay with her brother. Both were in very poor health. Martin, in great pain from his war injuries and loss of arm, was barely able to move. After working on the document throughout the day, Ellen retired for the evening. Martin could stay awake no longer, finally going to bed at 2 a.m. as the lawyer worked throughout the night on the divorce document.

Suddenly at 4 a.m., a violent pounding awoke Martin. Just before the lawyer opened the door, Manse stormed in then rushed to where Martin was sleeping. "Walworth came in and walked quietly up to the foot of my bed," Martin recalled. "He kept his hand by his side. I was still lying in bed, watching him closely. He asked me, 'Where is my wife?' He kept questioning me. I told him to keep quiet and allow me to dress. He was very much excited. I arose and was putting on my pants, still keeping an eye on him closely. I suddenly jumped towards the door and drew it after me. He pursued and forced the door open. He had his pistol in his hand. He presented it at me, but I escaped behind a double arch that was in the hall. People then came rushing to the spot. The lawyer had rung the bell and this gathered them. In a few seconds, a policeman came and arrested him."

Ellen sought a divorce on the grounds of cruel and inhumane treatment. Manse had allowed the divorce to proceed by default and took no action. His erratic behavior continued. In March 1871, he announced he was leaving the Roman Catholic Church. (His children were being raised as devote Catholics since both he and Ellen had converted and were wed in the church in the ceremony performed by his brother Father Clarence.) Manse told newspapers he no longer believed in the dogma of papal infallibility and would revert to being a Protestant like his late father. He also wrote his sister Mrs. Backus a letter threatening her and family with death if she failed to return $200 worth of property he declared belonged to himself. He indicated his book sales were not as he had hoped, and he needed $200 for advertisements to make his book a financial success. One of his letters to her is as follows.

*My Dear Sister:*

*"I have conceived the great secret of my existence. I was not born as men are, but was let down from heaven in a basket. All who have preceded me are imposters. I am the true Messiah. It will cause a great commotion on the earth when I am summoned,*

*for I shall be a soldier-king, and live in heaven—the home of my Father-God.*

*"You, of course, are not merely my sister, but during our terrestrial intercourse you have manifested such kindness for me that I shall make you one of the queens of the earth. * * * Keep this secret until I am announced by the sound of 10,000 trumpets, then fall down and worship me, for I am M.T. Walworth, the true and eternal son of God."*

The divorce was finalized April 8, 1871, with Manse to provide financial support for Ellen and the children. The court also awarded sole custody of the children to Ellen—rare at that time—due to Manse's abuse. Only when Manse learned the divorce included a clause to force him to pay alimony and child support did he begin to fight. Then he began writing numerous threatening letters to Ellen. He was especially irate about having to pay attorneys' fees and accusing Ellen of causing delays. To avoid paying alimony and child support, Manse had his lawyer make a motion in Supreme Court to open the judgement due to default and set aside decree. However, that motion never went to court because both Ellen and Manse eventually agreed to a compromise and made a modification in the decree on July 31, 1871 to remove his financial support, according to the *Marshall County Republican* newspaper. The stipulation also granted Manse monthly visits with the children.

Despite being able to see his children, Manse decided to stay away and continue writing menacing letters to Ellen. In fact, Manse never even saw their youngest child Sarah, a sickly infant born in June 1871 who died the following year in January 1872. The entire time Manse was writing the letters below, Ellen was recuperating from poor health and caring for her sick newborn. His letters mention legal delays on her part, while his thoughts focus only on himself and his money.

The children (circa 1873): Frank reclines on the floor. Ruby holds a sailor doll (middle left) while seated next to Nelly. Mansfield Tracy Jr. (top right) stands next to Clara. The Saratoga Springs History Museum.

*"Why do you not sign the papers with your lawyer says he sent to you? Is it not an honorable settlement, and was it not signed by me promptly? I waited weeks and weeks patiently, but your lawyer said the doctors wouldn't allow you to attend any business or sign it, and now, with the most marvelous breach of good faith, your lawyer has ruthlessly and treacherously gone to*

*the Trust Company which, by settlement, the lawyers
stipulated should be left along. If you incited him to
this breath of faith, you met a most signal failure. Are
you, his instigator, two-faced also? I made you some
offers to get to my work, and gave you about $250. As
God is my judge I never receive the document, which I
would have abided by; but now I will never make such
an agreement. Already $250 of my precious money
gone to my lawyer."*

Manse's latest work was hot off the presses:
*"Delaplaine, or, the Sacrifice of Irene."* It was met with
disdain in *Harper's Magazine* in September 1871. "If
it is intended as a novel, it is the wildest, craziest,
freakiest, maddest performance that an untrained
imagination, we should hope, ever put on paper.
Mr. Walworth has talents of no mean order. Will
not some kind friend show him how to use them?"

The tale starts with a 15-year-old boy being dragged off to prison in Sing Sing. The boy bites the hand of his captor to the bone to free himself and escapes his captors on a yacht in a river. The boy travels to foreign ports and becomes "a story of Baron Munchausen and Arabian Nights in about equal quantities; of marvelous military adventure; of magic, of astrology, of Persian shahs and Persian women inextricably intermixed." Letters to Ellen continued.

"Jesus God! aren't you going to sign the agreement your lawyer sent you? You are a demon, keeping me from success by wasting the precious dollars and tormenting me after a settlement has been agreed upon. Great God, woman, let me go to my work. The hardest time for 'Delaplaine' is here. In six weeks the fate of the book is told. Ellen Hardin, sing this paper which you agreed to sign. Great God, are you going to allow that crafty lawyer to get your name and to get my name as the author of 'Warwick,' to spread his name before the American public as a divorce lawyer? For, as sure as God is in heaven, if this agreement isn't signed I will place the fact before the public, but that is not my only resource; there is murder and suicide also! I waited six weeks time, but throw 'Delaplaine' into the ditch, reopen the divorce and sue for my children, unless you sign the agreement, and will devote the rest of my lift to fighting in the courts, and with murder and suicide in the end."

During her later life, Ellen became a prominent author in her own right. Manse's statement above may indicate that Ellen helped him either write or edit his books since he alludes to a possibility of adding her name as coauthor of *"Warwick."* No change was made to include her name on the book. It remains unknown why Manse brought up that issue. The newspapers of the day left blank spaces to remove some of Manse's more disturbing language from readers even though the complete letters were read aloud in court.

### July 8, 1871

*"Your lawyer asked another adjournment today. I cannot hold out longer. The pistols are loaded. If you succeed in getting the $950 from the trust estate of my father I shall shoot you, stamp out your life with my boot, and shoot myself if your mother is not near. If she is near I will use the second shot on her body and the third on myself, behind the ear. Why? Murder for $959, you ask? Why? Because you robbed me of my young; and now, in my miserable agony, on the loss of all that makes life tolerable, you remorselessly seek to knock from under a despairing wretch the last plank on which he can succeed. I went to Judge Barbour's to kill you; that door chain alone saved you. If you do not sign the papers your lawyer says he sent you to sign, and which your sickness alone prevented you from signing, I shall shoot you. You are dealing with a despairing, demoniacal murderer, or whatever despair makes a man. Sign ___ quick."*

It is easy to imagine the terror that Ellen must have experienced receiving such letters and threats. She had been a victim of domestic violence for decades—subject to fists, foul language, threats, erratic mood swings and more. Ellen and others knew Manse was certainly capable of acting out his murderous venting. Manse was known always to carry at least one pistol during the entire time she lived with him.

Their eldest child Frank was very close to his mother and tried to protect her from Manse. But Manse turned his abuse on Frank. Therefore, Frank temporarily moved to Kentucky to live with his uncle Lem, then a 30-year-old attorney.

Ellen's brother Lemuel Smith Hardin (1900). Although he became a lawyer, he gained more prominence for his dairy achievements and writing about agriculture. He won a cash award for an essay on Jersey cattle in 1875. Public domain photo.

HARDIN'S MILK-COOLER.

Lem's refrigerated invention to make butter: "A Method of Cooling Milk," (1876), *The American Agriculturist.*

167

*Saturday Night*

"I have just come from the lawyer's office. He says the agreement had not been signed and returned from Saratoga. _____ _____ you. Sign it and let me out of the expenses of the law. May _____ _____ the expenses of the law that are beggaring me! _____ _____ you. Your are planning some other evasion of your plighted word. Beware of me. _____ _____ you. I am dangerous. Listen to the murderer's hiss, and beware of me! You robbed me of my children and you want to rob me of my pittance. I am watching you with a hawk's eye and a despairing heart. Woman, why in God's name don't you sign the papers? The pistol is lying beside me loaded that will relive me from starvation and hell, and like a flaming demon I will scatter your brains. I am in earnest, _____ _____ you. Do the words sound tame on paper? Hog's _____, I will murder you for depriving me of my sweet, darling money. Hist! hist! hist! Le that ring through your _____ inhuman ears. The broken-hearted wretch will drag his torturer with him to hell."

*July 17, 1871*

"You _____ dishonorable _____. $200 more of the precious money gone to my lawyer. I cannot get into a situation where I can start afresh, and every delay causes loss, and the plank is riven under my feet and I am on the verge of beggary and desperation every hour. Whey do not you sign and give me a chance in life? I signed promptly. Why must this___ extortion of money for every adjournment go on? Don't you *know that your lawyer is charging you for every delay? Oh! I am crazy for just a few dollars to push my book 'Delaplaine' into success, and 'Delaplaine' is dying—dying! Two years more of my life wasted! Oh! ____ on Calvary____ but do not think the last cry means weakness; as, by the _____ ____, in wasting my time you have armed me. May _____ ____ ____ you. I revoke every promise I made you. I do not revoke my legal agreement. I stand by it as I do by every honorable agreement I ever made. It is your lawyer that played me false. This last trick of your lawyer, that it is necessary to make a stipulation that I will not break my engagement, is frivolous. Why didn't he think of it before" I do not care a ____; but put it in 50 times if you like; but hurry up, and stop this useless waste of money, since the first day I entered Charles M. Whitney's office. Eternal ____, can't we get it signed? He told me the lawyer had put the money stipulation into the agreement of his own option; and even Jude Barbour says to me that Whitney is a Yankee puppy, making out of the misery and patience and agonies of others, delay and pay, and to get it before the public in the courts; and I am ____ sure he is pursuing the course to get it there. I agreed with Judge Barbour to relinquish all nearly to you but $200, and Whitney never sent the agreement to me, according to promise. He is a ____ ___ liar; he never sent it to me. Hurry up for ___ ____ sake ___ ___ you. You are a fool."*

169

What neither Ellen nor her lawyer knew during this time was that Manse had big plans for his book *"Delaplaine."* His immense ego and desire for fame no doubt prompted him to send a copy of the book (written in English) as a gift to the Shah of Persia (Iran) Naser al-Din Shah Qajar. It must have cost Manse a pretty penny to send that book halfway around the world. Although Naser al-Din, an

Naser al-Din Shah Qajar (1831–1896). Wikimedia Commons.

avid photographer and painter, was familiar with the English language, he was not fluent. Apparently Manse thought it would be a good way to promote of his book, which contained Persian elements, by reaching out to the Shah. The Shah reciprocated the gift by bestowing Manse with a gold saber adorned with pearls like the one worn by Iranian Crown Prince Abbas Mirza (1789–1833), a military leader whose exploits were depicted in *"Delaplaine."* This sword (valued at $3,500) was described along with a promotion of the book in a San Francisco newspaper in January 1873. The article stated that the sword was a given as a token of appreciation for Manse's "historical accuracy and his brilliant description" of

Abbas Mirza. Manse stated that he intended to loan the sword for a year to display in the state library in Albany. This example shows what great lengths and expense Manse would take to promote his book. Ellen received more letters, showing what she endured.

*July 28, 1871*

*"Again today I have been to my lawyer. He says the papers to be signed by you are still in Saratoga. You are delaying, ____ of hell. Another adjournment to be paid for and the pennies scarce! The hopeless wretch grasps his pistol! You take the hopeless author this last hope. Vile ____ avaricious wretch, I grasp the deadly weapon for both of us. Stand off that property! You robbed me of everything sweet n life and of peace, and I want to wreak a dying vengeance on you if you do not relinquish your grasp on the only thing. ____ ____ you, you can appreciate my money. Sign the papers you agreed to sign long, long, long ago, and I will let you go, ____ dragging my heartstrings after you. But let go my sweet darling precious money. Too late I have learned that money is the hope of life and that for industrious poverty there is no home, no hope no success in life, no love of children; and I clutch the money with a demon's clutch, with a murderer's clutch and I would gladly murder for it and die. Sign the papers which you agreed to sign, ____. You have miscalculated Mansfield Tracy Walworth as others have done. You will awake to the reality when you beggar me and the bullet crashes through your skull*

171

*and through mine. Stand off ___ ___ you! I asked you*
*to do nothing which your lawyers have not stipulated*
*for, ___ ___ you, false, cold mean-hearted ___."*

He later instructed his attorney to draft an agreement for Ellen to sign to waive her rights to take him to court in the future in any financial disputes. Ellen refused to sign it. Below is a letter from Manse to Ellen after their divorce was finalized.

*Publication House, Carlton & Co.*
*Aug. 27*
*"Sign this paper and I will trouble you no further.*
*The devil says to me, you fool, she wants to beggar*
*you; she wants two-thirds since her father died;*
*she had kicked you out like a dog; she does not care*
*a groat whether you succeed or not' she means to*
*torment you about that property, because she is a*
*___ woman—a thief, a traitoress. Now sign this*
*paper, and I will try to bring this tortured brain once*
*more down to literary work. My lawyer says, she will*
*never sign anything that you want her to because she*
*gloats in torturing you. ___ you, Ellen Hardin.*
*It is in me to succeed at books if you leave me alone*
*and take the apprehension of lawsuits form me. Sign*
*this paper or a tortured author will kill you, by ___.*
*Why did you make me give up my children to you*
*and make no fight for them? Because I thought the*
*trust property would be left to me and that I could*
*succeed as an author. My lawyer says, she says I*

172

*am a fool; that she hates me; that you say you will
do nothing that I want you to do just to keep you
uneasy, and that your brain cannot bend to literary
work; she knows that if you succeed her affidavits
must be perjuries before the world. Now, sign this
paper, or I will murder you. I do not believe in any
God, but I believe there is a devil, and that devil is
you. Why in the name of common sense, after you
robbed me of the sweetness of life, do you not leave
me in undisturbed possession of the property, so that
I can stay in New York and work? Here industry
accomplishes wonders, even in the mere profession
of authorship. Sign this paper as a guarantee. What
did Whitney mean when he said there would be
more trouble about the property—that the Hardin's
ride will not allow them to contend about this little
property? In the name of God, when I gave you my
children for money, am I not allowed to live in peace,
when I would sell my soul for it? Oh, money is as
sweet to the Hardins as anybody else; but there is not
one of them who has courage to murder for money
as I have, and I will if I am not left in peace with
this two-thirds; for when that goes my last plank of
ambition will be taken from me and I will murder.
So hard, so hard is an author's fate."*

(The following text is the agreement that Manse
wanted Ellen to sign)

*"I promise before God to abstain against all
lawsuits or take any of the property. I am satisfied*

173

*with one-third which he has relinquished for my
relief. I know he has well enough to carry on his mind
from remorseless children, without my crippling him
by lawsuits for money. Sign this paper to give me
mental rest, necessary for literary work. I will not
approach his trust again or enter any court so long
as I receive one-third trust property."*

In the following weeks, Ellen moved around for
brief periods to live with Martin, her sister-in-law's
family and Father Clarence before finally returning
with her mother and children to the family home in
Saratoga. The only male staying with her for her
protection against Manse was teenaged Frank, a
slender youth who stood 5-feet, 8 inches tall. In
contrast, Manse had a more powerful stature. A
longtime weight-lifter who used dumbbells and was
vain about his personal appearance, Manse stood
at 5 feet 11 inches.

Eventually both Manse and Ellen agreed to a
stipulation in the divorce regarding support. She was
to provide for herself and the children—without any
money from Manse—except for $500 share she received
from the Chancellor's estate. All proceeds he received
from his work as an author he kept for himself.

Ever intellectually gifted and resourceful, Ellen set
about turning the family home (where she lived with
her children and elderly mother) into a girls' boarding
and day school. Her inspiration for this business venture

arose from her desire to educate her children and earn a living. "To facilitate the education of her children she collected classes and engaged the best teachers to be had in Boston and New York to conduct special studies in music and art. These classes finally developed into a very successful boarding and day school, and she enlarged the old homestead for its accommodation, letting the house during the summer vacations for a family hotel, and building herself a modes cottage on the grounds," noted *American Monthly Magazine*.

Manse continued his reign of terror against Ellen after the divorce. Today, it would constitute stalking and harassment, but back then there was little she could do but hold her head high and continue to carry on. It made no difference to Manse that they were divorced. He continued to abuse and humiliate her. He sent her obscene and threatening letters. When she refused to receive his letters, he disguised his handwriting to trick her into opening them. Frank tried to intercept the letters and confront his father. Manse, however, only divided his hatred between Ellen and Frank. Once Manse threatened to rent a house next to Ellen's school and live there with a mistress to cause a scandal to her reputation and at the school.

According to Judge Barbour, Manse paid to take out a slanderous advertisement in the *Home Journal* (a N.Y. newspaper that regularly printed his articles) to insult Ellen. The ad stated: "There exists at Saratoga a young ladies' school, named after the celebrated author, Mansfield Tracy Walworth. It is kept by

Mrs. __ Hardin (her maiden name). Mr. Walworth has presented the institution with a rare collection of shells and fossils (things which he did not own)."

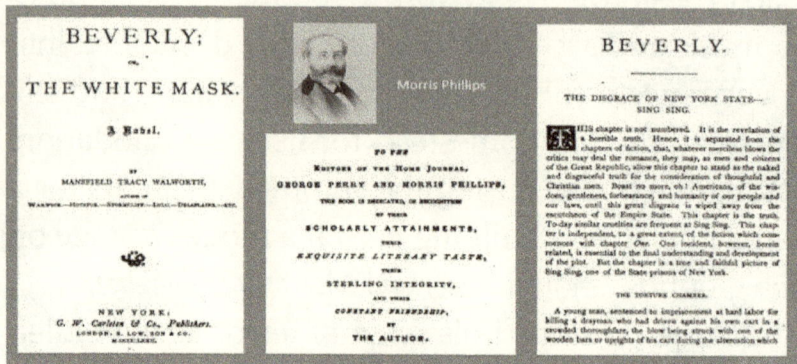

Manse penned a dedication to the *Home Journal* editors George Perry and Morris Phillips (who published his slander against Ellen) and recognized them for their "exquisite literary taste" and friendship. Photo: The New York Public Library.

Manse diffused some of his energy from Ellen into his latest novel: *"Beverly, or The White Mask,"* published in 1872 in 422 pages. He wrote this book portraying himself as the hero amid an unhappy life. Focusing on an aspect of a N.Y. criminal law, the book was partially set in New York City and the Hudson River. As with his other works, it received mixed reviews.

• "It opens with a murder, and from this as a center, radiate the multitudinous and complicated incidents which make up the story. It is a mass of mystery, intrigue, and crime, mixed with no inconsiderable skill, and well calculated to excite and disorder the mind. It is much to be regretted that this writer's really fine powers should be spent in so unworthy a service as this book represents."—*The Literary World*, April 1, 1872.

• "The keynote of the book is an introductory chapter disclosing the horrible barbarities and torture practices at Sing Sing. In the torture chamber the thumb-pully is still in operation, and the number of yearly 'pullied' there is 208. The revelation of the barbarities of this prison ought to make a sensation that will lead to a revolution in that prison, which is by all reports one of the most disgraceful in America."—*Hartford Courant*, June 1, 1872.

Guard at Sing Sing prison guardhouse (late 1800s). The New York Public Library.

• "Mr. Walworth's plots are unfathomable, because they are so grossly improbable and contradictory that no sane reader would dream of suggesting the true solution.. The wealth of the hero is greater an hundred-fold than that of Monte Cristo, and a conspicuous character is a 'dream-child,' who comes no one knows whence, and goes no one knows whither. It is suggested, however, that she is of supernatural origin, which my account for the clairvoyance which, with a dash of spiritualism, flavors the book. There is no individuality in the characters. They all talk after the same pattern. A more rubbishing book has not been printed this season…"—*The Charleston Daily News*, June 11, 1872.

Little did Manse know at that time, but he would never live to see another of his books published. It is ironic that topics he frequently wrote about—murder, violence, the rich, high society, shooting family members to death with bullets from pistols, trials, law and even Sing Sing—would all feature prominently in the tale of his miserable demise. His last letter to Ellen, which she received after his death, was written May 30, 1873.

Manse (1873). The New York Public Library.

*Seven o'clock in the Morning.*

*"Prepare yourself for the inevitable. I am getting over my wasting fever and shall be out of my room in a few days. I am going to call upon my children; my heart is starving for their caresses. Make the interview as easy and pleasant as possible. I cannot stay from them much longer. I will see them—peaceably if I can, or with a tragedy if I must. Their little faces haunt me, as they are mine. Popish cruelty must bend to the demand of a father's breast, or the Walworth name goes out in blood.*

*"Keep Frank Walworth out of my way. You have taught him to hate me, and his presence or obstruction*

in any way will only excite fatal exasperation. I want to see my little girl and come away peaceably. Beware that you do not in any way arouse the frenzy which you have known to exist since you left me. There is a reasonable way to deal with me. I shall have my rights under that decree, with no further legal delay or expense. I have conceded promptly every right under that decree, and not I am going out see my children, and you shall not bring them up to hate their loving father.

"Eliza Backus has written to me that you will do it if you can, from your associations with them; and then I shall shoot you and myself on those doorsteps, for I have nothing further to live for. I am a broken-hearted desperado. I admit it. Save this letter for lawyers and courts if you please. God is my lawyer; not the remorseless, brutal god that you and Eliza Backus and C.A. Walworth [his brother Clarence] worship, but that God who has planted love in my heart for my little girls, and that says to the tiger bereft of its young, 'Kill!' you are an infamous wretch to keep me for more than two years from the little hands and hearths that love me.

"Your only excuse was my poverty and misfortune. When Frank refused to speak to me in the streets of Saratoga, I said to myself, 'She is teaching them all to hate a broken-hearted father.' Then all is lost and the tragedy must come. When I know from the conduct of my little girls that you have taught them to hate me, that moment two pistol shots will ring about your *house—one slaying you, the other myself.*

*"I know that you have no personal fear, no more than I have, but we both must die when the discovery comes that you have estranged my young children from me. It is possible that you have not done so, and you shall have your life. If my little girls do not love me, then life is valueless, and I shall die with a feeling of luxury and rest to come; but you will have to attend me to the spirit land. The God of justice demands it. Therefore I say to you do right under that decree, then all may be well; but now my heart is agonized for my little children. If you had common sense you would know how to appreciate the danger."*

*Mansfield Tracy Walworth*

Manse, elegantly clad in dark a broadcloth coat and vest, a dress shirt with a white tie and plain gold studs and lavender trousers, took his last breaths shortly after 6:15 a.m. in room No. 267 at the Sturtevant House in New York City on June 3, 1873. He had been shot to death

Sturtevant House (1873). The New York Public Library.

with a pistol by his eldest son Frank (19) inside the youth's room at the six-story Sturtevant House at 29th and Broadway. His body lay on its side with

180

"The Walworth Parricide," (1873) by Thomas O'Kane, N.Y.

his head near a washstand next to a window and his feet near door. The chair, in which he had been sitting while talking to Frank, was broken and overturned.

Tired of the threatening letters to his mother and himself, Frank left Saratoga armed with his cousin's Colt revolver on a secret mission to confront Manse. He checked into the hotel on the preceding afternoon and left a calling card with a servant at his father's city residence in a boarding house on 4th Avenue near 54th Street.

## THREE O'CLOCK

I want to try and settle some family matters. Call at the Sturtevant House in an hour or two. If I am not there I will leave word at the office.

### FRANK H. WALWORTH

Frank waited throughout the day and into the morning, never sleeping, and sitting on his unmade bed anticipating his father's arrival. Finally, Manse came to the hotel at such an early hour that the clerk almost refused to show Manse up because he

181

thought Frank would be asleep. "Oh, he will see me," Manse replied, as a bellboy took up his calling card to Frank's room. With instructions to send Manse to the room, the bellboy heard the door barely close when the sound of four rapidly fired shots rang out. A commotion ensued. A night watchmen and a hotel steward rushed upstairs. A merchant in the next room jumped out of bed, ran over into the hallway and opened the door of Frank's room. Staggering back in horror, the merchant saw a large pool of blood around Manse's body. Then Frank, wearing a gray summer suit, calmly put the pistol in his pocket, took his hat from the bureau and leisurely walked away from the room to the telegraph office. He handed over a note to be sent to his uncle Martin Hardin, then newly married and living in Chicago with his wife.

*"The Walworth Parricide."*

## STURTEVANT HOUSE, New York
### Hardin, Chicago, Ill:

I have shot and killed father.

### FRANK H. WALWORTH

"Before the operator could recover from his astonishment, young Walworth had reached the hotel office counter, and bending over, asked the clerk, 'Where is the nearest police station?' The clerk answered, 'The 29th Precinct, in 30th Street, near 7th Avenue.' Frank Walworth then answered, 'I have killed my father in my room, and I am going to surrender myself to the police.' Then he walked out of the hotel," according to *The New York Times*, June 4, 1873. Hotel guests thronged the corridors as news spread of the sensational patricide. The Sturtevant was crowded with over 100 guests who had gathered there for a Grand Lodge meeting.

Frank confessed at the station. Police and a coroner rushed to the hotel room. They found Manse's calling card (written at the hotel and brought up by the bellboy) on the carpet where it had been tossed and crushed by Frank near the body. Four bullets had entered Manse's body, three were fatal. "One shot broke the right arm, one entered just below the right nipple of the breast, another at the left nipple, and the fourth and last crashed into the skull at the right ear, and entered

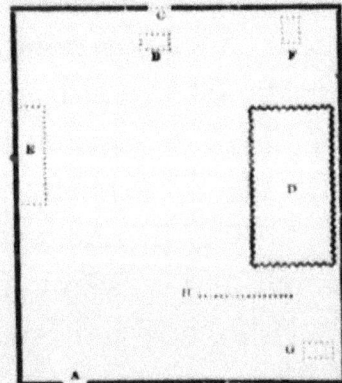

The annexed diagram will explain the scene of the tragedy:

A—Door.
B—Chair on which Frank H. Walworth was seated when the call boy entered.
C—Window looking toward Fifth avenue.
D—Bed.
E—Dressing table.
F—Stove.
G—Wash stand.
H—The corpse.

Crime scene from "The Sun," June 4, 1873.

183

the brain. There were powder marks surrounding the surface of the last wound. The letter written by young Walworth on Monday, and left at his father's house, was found in the inside breast pocket of Mr. Walworth's coat. It had been pierced by the ball which entered his right breast, and was covered with blood." Police believed it was murder. It looked as though Frank allowed Manse to enter the room, sit on a chair and then Frank closed the door. Turning his back on the door, Frank shot at Manse, who staggered and fell forward onto Frank's shoulder when Frank fired the last shot into his father's head.

Frank provided a motive for the killing. He told police that he asked his father in the hotel room to stop threatening his mother and writing disgraceful letters. According to Frank, Manse agreed at first and then changed his mind, insulting the youth and Ellen. "I stepped forward, and he put his hand in his pocket as if to draw a pistol. Then I shot him. When the last shot was fired, he grappled with me. I have no regret regarding this matter, except that it will annoy my family and cause my dear mother anxiety."

Police arrested Frank and put him in cell No. 44 with a man sentenced to death for murder. As an be imagined, Ellen was frantic when she heard the news. She telegraphed an attorney/former judge to defend her son. "From dispatches received from Saratoga," the *Times* remarked, "it appears that Mrs. Walworth and her son have the entire sympathy of the community residents there, young Walworth sustaining a high character, while his father bore a reputation directly the reverse."

Three days after Manse's death, his remains arrived in Saratoga for burial at Greenridge Cemetery. The burial service was attended by Ellen and her son Tracy as well as Manse's siblings and brothers-in-law. Rev. Dr. Norman

Manse's body was brought by train from NYC to this Saratoga Railroad Depot. Saratoga Springs Public Library.

Camp, of the local Episcopalian Bethesda Church, administered the burial service. (Ellen's youngest surviving child was Tracy, named after his father, but went by his middle name. His father's funeral took place two weeks before Tracy's fifth birthday on June 19.)

The murder victim's remains had been in the ground for 48 hours when *The Daily Saratogian* backed Ellen and Frank. "Mansfield T. Walworth's character was pretty generally known here, and his name was held in contempt by all save such as may have been of like cut, while Mrs. Walworth and her family were universally respected," it declared June 9, 1873. The newspaper surmised that the killing wasn't an act of premeditation due to the youth's good character and temperament. "When the character of Mansfield Walworth is exposed and his atrocious treatment of his family is known, the tragedy will be better comprehended than it is at the present time outside of Saratoga."

At the time of his death, one of Manse's stories, written as a satire of Ellen, was being published as a serial in *The New York Weekly*. Called *"Married in Mask,"* the work was published posthumously in 1888 as a book under the copyright of A.L. Burt, publisher. It is unknown if Ellen or the children received any compensation from this work.

This chapter of Ellen's life was one of intense suffering. Although she was freed from further abuse, her life turned completely upside-down. Her primary concern was to help and protect her son Frank. She and other family members insisted that Frank had not murdered his father in cold blood, but acted in self-defense when he thought his father was moving his hand to his vest to retrieve a pistol. But Manse had no weapon.

Ellen's private life and family was to become the subject of intense interest nationwide. Sensational headlines shrieked of the horror of *"Patricide."* The degrading domestic violence and injuries she experienced were no longer closely guarded secrets. Manse's dirty laundry was aired far and wide before, during and after Frank's murder trial. Some newspapers wrote lies to smear her reputation—some declared she had been pregnant with Frank before her marriage to Manse, or that she was a disloyal citizen/Confederate spy. She never responded to any false allegations. However, the *Evening Star* wrote on June 16, 1873 *"The Slanders upon Mrs. Walworth"* to set the record straight.

Despite sympathetic reports about what Ellen and her children had endured under the hands of Manse, a sentiment prevailed across the country that no child should be freed of guilt for murdering a parent. There was concern of setting a bad precedent should Frank be set free. His consistent lack of remorse and justification of the crime, bordering on arrogance, hurt his cause.

"The friends of young Walworth, who murdered his father, are sparing no pains (or expense, perhaps) to manufacture public sympathy for that interesting youth, but they may overdo it. There are people who will believe that Mansfield Walworth got tipsy and abused and insulted his wife, but the friends of that lady are trying to make of the deceased (who seems to have been a gentleman of culture, occasionally debased by drink) an incarnate fiend or a madman," noted the *Evening Star*, shortly after the killing.

The Walworth slaying became a "celebrated murder case" that provided endless news coverage and articles speculating on different aspects of the case. A few days after the killing, the *Evening Star*, discussed the idea circulating that Frank would escape hanging for the assassination of his father

187

due to his influential family connections. However, disapproval of the act was rising. "The New York papers, by the way, are instructing to a healthy public opinion in regard to this atrocious parricide. The *Tribune* calls the murder 'selfish, unnatural, brutal.' The *Sun* declares that 'the fact that the father was a bad man affords not the slightest justification; there is nothing of self-defense about this act.' *The Evening Post* thinks that there is no palliation for the crime of a boy who comes 150 miles with murderous intent and slays his father, and the *Herald* calls young Walworth a 'monstrous offender,' and preaches a sermon on the general and alarming disrespect shown of late years by children for their parents."

Ellen's family and in-laws rallied around both Frank and herself. Soon after the murder, Lem (by then a prominent Louisville lawyer) hurried over with a letter he received a few weeks earlier from Manse threatening to kill her and Frank. It was hoped this letter would help Frank's legal defense.

Negative press articles appeared about Manse. "As a citizen, he [Manse] was under the charge of disloyalty during the dark hours of

**TELEGRAPH NEWS.**

Last Night's Report.

**FRANK H. WALWORTH.**

Personal and Legal Efforts to Palliate the Terrible Crime.

Second Day of the Boy-Murderer's Trial—The Wife and Mother on the Witness Stand—An Insane Letter of Deceased Read as Evidence—The Boy's Note to his Uncle, the Day Before the Tragedy, Etc., Etc.

NEW YORK, June 26. — The Walworth trial was resumed and the prisoner was surrounded by his mother, Mrs. Chancellor Walworth, and numerous other relatives and friends.

THE DEFENSE.

A. Ebert, first witness for the defense, occupied the room next to rhat where the mur-

*Evening Courier & Republic* (Buffalo, N.Y.), June 27, 1873.

his country's peril; and as a man, his reputation where he was best known was seriously damaged. Had he been disposed to a suitable improvement of his talents, he might have filled a mediocre position in life and reached decent respectability. Multitudes do this who are no more gifted than he, but such was not his disposition. He chose his course in life. He gratified his base

Illustration of Frank Walworth, *Harper's Weekly*, June 28, 1873.

inclinations, and he has met a result which however horrible and unnatural, is still the fruit of his own conduct. Had he done his duty he would never have become the victim of a parricide," by Macaulay (a popular column written under a pen name for Rev. Washington Frothingham) in the *Rochester Democrat*, June 1873.

Ellen took on a prominent role as a courtroom spectator and witness when Frank was charged with murdering Manse in the sensational trial that began June 25, 1873 in the Court of Oyer and Terminer—a criminal court composed of a Supreme Court Justice and judges who had jurisdiction over felony cases punishable by life imprisonment or death. It was abolished in 1895 when its jurisdiction was transferred to the

Illustration of criminal court in NYC in the *"Manual of the Corporation of City of New York,"* 1870.

N.Y. Supreme Court. "The prisoner looked perfectly unconcerned and indifferent. His mother, dressed in deep mourning and closely veiled, sat beside him, occasionally holding a handkerchief to her eyes. She was accompanied by another son [Tracy], a boy of about 12, and by several ladies who were evidently friends or relatives of the family," noted *The New York Times*. Frank's uncles (Gen. Martin, Rev. Dr. Backus and Father Clarence) also attended along with Justice Barbour.

The courtroom was filled each day of the trial to overflowing. The court heard from the prosecution that Frank must be found guilty of a deliberate murder, how Frank had traveled over 100 miles to meet his father and displayed no emotion either before or after the killing. The defense contended that the teenager had turned into "a sullen moody lad" because of Manse's constant brutal treatment of his mother, which had distorted his mind and driven him to commit the act. Mention was made of introducing to the court as evidence Manse's threatening letters that he sent to Ellen, even up to five letters in a single day.

The trial was presided by Judge Noah Davis, seated on a wide chair. "Judge Davis does not look like a judge. He has much more the air of a well-to-do merchant, who, having acquired a substantial fortune, had retried. There is very little that is lawyer-like in his appearance. He is a short, thick-set red-faced man with a quiet face, small eyes, but occasionally irritable manner. He was dressed scrupulously in black," wrote the N.Y.

N.Y. Supreme Court Judge Noah Davis, in office from July 1870 to December 1872. Wikimedia Commons.

correspondent for the *Boston Post*. Some 300 people were summoned for the jury pool, but only 138 showed up. "As for the jury, they seemed rather a dull, sleeping-looking set—more evenly taken from the ignorant class, I should say, than yours. In the most moving scenes which transpired—and some were certainty calculated to produce emotion—I saw no indication of feeling in the jury box."

On the next day of the trial, Frank appeared as nonchalant as ever as he sat beside Ellen, Tracy and two of his sisters. Frank's relatives testified about his good character. Next Ellen testified. She described

her relationship with Manse. The day before the killing, she spoke to Frank at their Saratoga home and was unaware he left for New York until she was told he left suddenly. She went to his room and discovered an empty envelope with Manse's handwriting on the outside. Becoming alarmed, she immediately telegraphed Clarence and Judge Barbour. Then two of Manse's recent threatening letters were introduced as evidence and read to the court. The defense maintained the letters proved Frank was not in his right mind when the shooting occurred, and Manse was not a loving father lured into a trap by his son.

During the trial, Ellen sent her eldest surviving daughter and namesake on a trip abroad with her uncle, Father Clarence. (Frank was supposed to be on the trip but instead was on trial for murder.) So, 14-year-old Ellen (Nellie) Hardin Walworth put her studies on hold for a year at Kenwood Convent of the Sacred Heart in Albany. Escaping a public stigma, she sailed for Europe in late June. Despite her focus on the trial, Ellen encouraged Nellie's writing abilities by suggesting the girl pen long letters home that would be compiled into a journal. The girl's letters were shrewdly passed along by Ellen to be published as an ongoing series by *The Sunday Morning Press* (Albany). By the time Nellie returned home a year later, she already had acquired good reputation as a writer. In fact, the letters became a book by Nellie published in 1877 called, *"An Old World as Seen through Young Eyes; or Travels Around the World."* The book was dedicated: *"To My Mother, Mrs. Ellen Hardin Walworth with Unmeasured Love and Respect, I dedicate this account of My Travels."*

Ellen and Frank talking in the Tombs (nickname for the Lower Manhattan jail (1873). The New York Public Library.

On the third day of the trial, the prosecution objected to more of Manse's letters being used as evidence. However, the judge allowed portions of those to be read that contained threats. Nineteen letters were accepted. One letter from Manse to Ellen contained only gunpowder and bullets.

Ellen was recalled to the stand. Under questioning, she said she told Frank about one beating she received from Manse and showed bruises on her arm. "'There was a look of extreme suffering,' said she, 'which I had never seen before, and it alarmed me so much that I never told him again of anything of the kind. He said very little, however, and I can only remember his saying, 'This must not be.' He was very quiet and very pallid,'" noted *The New York Times*, June 28, 1873. Ellen left the courtroom when Manse's letters were read aloud, while Frank looked downcast with this hands over his face. "Some of the letters were greeted

193

with laughter, their profanity and billingsgate being often absurd," the *Times* remarked. "One of the insane productions avowed the singular doctrine that the whole American people had decided that the courts were now so corrupt that a man had to kill everybody to obtain justice."

Manse's letters to Ellen called her numerous names including an avaricious slut and a pig-headed, mule demon. He called her thief, adding that he would hush her woman's rights pretenses with a bullet. He threatened to kill her many times. Some letters accused Ellen of "indiscriminate infidelity." Manse also suggested Frank was conceived outside of wedlock. The reading of 19 of Manse's letters only served to inflame interest in the trial. For nearly two months, over 1,000 newspapers articles appeared in the country with detailed coverage of the Walworth family murder. Even *The Freeman's Journal* in Ireland carried an account of it on June 20, 1873 called *"Another American Tragedy."*

An Indiana newspaper, the *Marshall County Republican* contained reaction to the letters from Manse's supporters. His friends "say he had but too much grounds for the charges against his wife. They say that he sustained improper [sexual] relations with her himself, before their marriage, and that only upon this ground would their parents' consent to their union. This latter fact is the basis of the slur upon Frank's birth, which incited the young man to take summary vengeance upon its author."

## THE WALWORTH TRAGEDY.

**Progress of the Young Patricide's Trial in New York.**

**The Story as Told by the Mother and Wife.**

**The Fatal Letters — Why Frank Shot His Father.**

**Mrs. Walworth Deserted by Her Husband and then Abused.**

The Mother and Wife.

NEW YORK, June 27.—The Walworth trial is in progress. Mrs. Ellen Hardin Walworth being sworn said: I am the mother of Frank Walworth : was married to M. T. Walworth, in St. Peter's church, Saratoga Springs, in 1852, on July 29th, and resided at the Chancellor's House, which my mother now owns ; lived there until the summer of 1861. The Chancellor's family

## WALWORTH TRIAL.

Testimony of Witnesses in the Walworth Trial.

Mrs. Walworth's Testimony in the Case.

Production of two Letters in Evidence.

The Last Threatening Letter to Mrs. Walworth.

WALWORTH TRIAL.

New York, June 26.—The trial of Frank H. Walworth, for killing his father, Mansfield Tracy Walworth, was resumed this morning. About thirty friends and relations of the prisoner were in the court room in deep mourning. The first witness called was for

## THE WALWORTH PARRICIDE.

The Meeting Between the Mother and Son at the Tombs Yesterday.

**What the Prisoner's Defence Will Be.**

Interviews with Ex-Assistant District Attorney Garvin and Mr. Charles O'Conor.

**AN UNFORTUNATE MARRIAGE.**

Further Particulars of the Unhappy Wedded Life of Mrs. Walworth.

*Left: Star Tribune* (Minneapolis), June 27, 1873; center: *Leavenworth Daily Commercial* (Kans.) June 27, 1873; right: *New York Daily Herald*, June 5, 1873.

The *Interior Journal* (Ky.) newspaper dubbed Manse one of the greatest blackguards to escape public execution. "When the news first flashed across the country, in common with everyone, we condemned the act of parricide, and felt that it was one which deserved the severest punishment of the law;' but since the letters of Mansfield Tracy Walworth to the mother of his children has been made public, we can but feel that if young Walworth deserves hanging, it is because he did not take the life of the fiend who was daily tormenting his mother, sooner."

Under the headline *"Idiocy as a Profession,"* the *New York Times* printed a scathing reaction to the letters. It declared:

*"...but that a fat man should sit down in the privacy of his hotel to write such amazing rubbish at the rate of three or four letters per day, is absolutely staggering to*

195

the sane imagination. Mr. Walworth is dead, and it is eminently proper to speak as well of him as truth will permit. Were he, however, in full possession of his bodily health and mental mucilage, it would be only paying him a tribute he deserved to treat him as the most successful and incontestable idiot of the age ... it was not as a mere writer of books that he sought distinction, for he must have been perfectly aware that not even the literature of trunk-linings would accept him. He wrote novels to demonstrate his claim to preeminent idiocy and it is an idiot that he is to be judged.

"That this idiot was addicted to the infamy of writing filthy, blasphemous, and cowardly letters to a woman, in order to terrify her into giving him money, has been sufficiently established. This fact, nevertheless, has little to do with the question of the guilt of the young man now on trial for his life for having slain him...it is not our habit to make any comments upon a trial during its progress. But since the public sense of decency has been shocked by the production of these Walworth letters, it is quite proper to express an opinion upon the writer of them, even although he is dead."

The *Chicago Daily Tribune* weighed in on the scandalous testimony in a lengthy article called "The Walworth Letters."

"The letters themselves form a series of the vilest and most obscene vituperation, and, under the circumstances which surround their conception, they are curious and remarkable. If they were the production of an ignorant and illiterate man, controlled by brutal passions and unrestrained by personal culture or respectable associations, they would be dismissed as vile evidences of a viscous nature. But they were written by a man of education and position, the son of a Chancellor of high name, the pet of a very high-toned class of New York society, a fashionable author, and a person who passed for a gentleman in the eyes of the world.

"They are addressed to a wife, who comes of good family, and has enjoyed the advantages of culture. Yet they are filled with a succession of blasphemous and disgusting epithets, of filthy and low-flung expressions of degraded and repulsive sentiments which the lowest pimp would scarcely address to his mistress.

"It is rare that any man reaches a depth of degradation in which he is willing to put on paper the indelible evidence of a mind sunk in the very dregs of infamy, as this man Walworth, a writer in the Home Journal, and, for a time, a sort of social lion, has done. Whether the letters that have been printed were the expression of a man maddened with grief; or of a mind that had lost its balance; or of a deliberate purposed to seek revenge for assumed wrongs; or of an intention to intimidate the woman to whom they were addressed, they bear, in any case, the stamp of moral degradation that will go far to enforce the doctrine of total depravity.

*"Underlying the wicked intent and disgusting blasphemy of these letters is evidence of a sordid nature that renders them more revolting, if possible, than they could have been otherwise. This society man and author, this representative of a good family, this type of gentleman, breaths forth his poisonous and withering blasphemy, and threatens death to his wife and children, not because of any pangs of separation or consciousness of disgrace, but because his wife's delay in signing the papers of separation has cost him a couple of hundred dollars. Money is the burden of his lament, and its loss is what mainly prompts him to threaten murder.*

*"He gloats fiendishly over the thought of gratification at crushing his wife's skull, 'gutting' his son, thereby blotting the name of Walworth out of existence, and then killing himself—all because of the additional cost of lawyers' fees that might have been saved. He curses his father's name because he was left only an income, not a fee-simple interest in the estate. Altogether, there has probably never been written evidence of a more infamous, groveling, and vicious character than Mansfield Tracy Walworth has left."*

Not only in New York City where the trial was taking place, was there intense interest in the Walworths, but also at their hometown Saratoga. People couldn't help but pass by the family estate without stopping to stare. Everyone, both residents and visitors alike, constantly spoke about the trial. Everyone had an

198

opinion to share. Although the family was held in high regard, including Frank, most people were aghast at the crime. Some believed Frank should hang for the crime. Others opposed capital punishment as the right punishment given Manse's domestic violence.

As the trial continued, various relatives, friends, associates and household staff were called who attested to either the good character of Frank or his father. Medical testimony was introduced indicating Frank had suffered from a past head injury and epileptic seizures. On the morning of July 3, 1873, the courtroom was packed as the prosecution made its final argument. Jurors were told they should only consider if Mansfield Tracy Walworth died as a result of willful and deliberate act by Frank no matter how vile and degraded the deceased was. The judge provided a lengthy instruction to the jury during which he discussed Manse's letters to Ellen and other family members. "A party who receives letters, however insulting, has not the legal right to commit an assault in consequence of it. Assault and battery cannot be justified by the most opprobrious and abusive words; and whether those words are oral or written, the law will not justify the party of receives them in inflecting personal chastisement even upon the writer," the judge declared, "...however bad these letters, however wicked and brutal and cruel, the writer had not forfeited his life because he had penned them; nor had the party who received them, nor any friend of his, been clothed by law with the power to pass sentence of death and execute the sentence because of the character of those letters."

While the jury deliberated, Ellen stayed in the courtroom with Frank, newspaper reporters and other spectators. One reporter later stated that most spectators believed the defense failed to prove insanity, but rather a case of cold-blooded murder. After about four hours, the jury of 12 men returned. "When the verdict was read of murder in the second degree, the prisoner received the blow without a change of countenance, and when, at a nod from the clerk, the jury sat down, he, too, resumed his seat and restlessly loosened his necktie. His mother turned toward him one look of affection, as his wearied eye caught hers, she turned the look into a smile, to which the prisoner wearily responded," *The Baltimore Sun*, July 4, 1873. Newspapers across the national voiced their approval of the verdict.

Sentencing took place July 6, 1873 with Ellen and other supporters surrounding Frank. Judge Davis spoke. "Walworth, I have never been called upon in my life to perform a more painful duty than the one which devolves upon me now," said the judge, adding that the evidence fully justified the verdict. "...I cannot conceive what motives you could have had in preparing yourself, as you did, with a pistol loaded, coming to New York, seeking an interview with your father, and almost immediately shooting him down, except upon the idea that you had deliberately determined that his life should be terminated by your

Frank during the trial (1873). The New York Public Library.

hand. ...Your poor mother had indeed great cause to feel not only grieved merely, but ashamed and indignant at the long course of outrages toward her and toward his family; but, bad as he was, you were not to be the avenger of those wrongs. He had done nothing to forfeit his life, even to the laws of his country, and least of all had he done anything to forfeit his life at the hands of his own and eldest son. When I look back at that moment when you constituted yourself his executioner, and slew him in that room, with no one present but yourselves, I cannot but feel that death must have been more horrible than a thousand deaths in any other form. Called by you to your presence apparently for the purposes of a peaceful interview to settle family difficulties, invited to a seat in your room, and apparently almost instantly confronted with a weapon of death in his own son's hands, what thoughts must have rushed upon him at that moment, when he found that the person whom he expected had come to him for the purposes of a peaceful arrangement—what terrible thoughts must have rushed upon him when he received the leaden messenger of death in his bosom from the hands of his eldest boy? I shudder when I think of it, and I think you out to devote your whole life to repentance

201

such as God only can accept for so horrible a deed. The sentence of the Court is that you be imprisoned in the State Prison at Sing Sing at hard labor, for the full term of your natural life."

Inside Sing Sing Prison. The New York Public Library.

After the sentence was pronounced, Frank maintained his blasé demeanor. Taken back to be incarcerated at The Tombs municipal jail, Frank apparently told a deputy sheriff about being glad he didn't have to suffer through a long lecture from the Judge Davis. Two days later, he and 11 other criminals were to be transported to the Hudson River railroad depot in the journey to Sing Sing. Waiting outside Tombs in a carriage, Ellen asked for permission to have Frank ride with her to the rail station. Her request was refused. Instead Frank, manacled like the other prisoners, rode in prison van. He was handcuffed with another convicted murderer for the trip to Sing Sing.

"Young Walworth's broken-hearted mother traveled on a rear car of the same train. She could not bear to see handcuffs on her son, and as the latter from time to time received little encouraging notes from her through the medium of a kindly conductor...," recalled *The Brooklyn Daily Eagle* in

July 1882. When it came time to exchange his clothes for prison garb, Frank removed a pair of gold sleeve buttons that were weighed and measured before being locked away. Changing into a striped flannel prison uniform, Frank turned toward a fellow killer with whom he had been handcuffed to previously. "I feel as if I was going to play a game of baseball," Frank remarked cheerfully.

The next day, Ellen visited Frank at Sing Sing. She brought her daughters 13-year-old Clara and Reubena "Ruby" (age 6), son Tracy (age 5), and her aged mother. Only Ellen was allowed to see him through the grating of his cell door. She brought him a large basket of tuberoses adorned in the center with the initials F.H.

Within days of arriving at Sing Sing, a notorious maximum-security prison, the *Evening Star* complained about Frank receiving special treatment despite his life sentence to hard labor. "He is not to be placed on a level with the common convicts; not a bit of it, but is to be made 'chief clerk of the stock department,' where his labors will be wholly clerical and where he can look down with lofty disdain upon the poor devils who, while they have not attained his attitude in crime, are compelled to submit to the full rigor of their sentence."

Ellen didn't just walk away. Instead she took a very unusual step in trying to provide maternal care for her criminal son. She decided to live awhile with her youngest son Tracy in a boarding house near Sing Sing. She caused a sensation in a local Catholic church when she attended as a veiled lady in deep mourning. She also obtained other privileges for Frank. He was allowed to visit with her on a sofa in a front office. Then he was given a job as a clerk in a shoe department. The last exception to the rule she

Prisoners going to work. The New York Public Library.

obtained for Frank was that no visitors or strangers were allowed to see him while passing through the prison. Undoubtedly, Ellen pulled Walworth family strings to shield Frank from being treated like an ordinary prisoner.

The public and press frowned on this special treatment. "They make a hero of young Walworth because he is rich, handsome, intelligent and so engaging in his manners....We are asked to admire this noble youth, and express our regret that he should be chained to a vulgar convict of the common sort, and hurried off to Sing Sing, where he performs the onerous duties of assistant clerk in the shoe department; shut off, however, from the gaze of visitors so that his sensitive feelings may not be hurt. Before he became a parricide but a small portion of the world knew of or cared for him, and now they would have us pray that he may speedily be released from prison."—*The New York Times*, July 18, 1873.

Ellen returned to the Walworth mansion in

Saratoga in October. Her efforts shifted to winning support among prominent men in New York to secure a pardon for Frank.

By Dec. 6, 1873, Frank became ill with a pneumonia-like condition that paved the way for him to be transferred from Sing Sing to a less infamous state penitentiary in Auburn, N.Y. Evidently Ellen played a role in this.

"Just after the convicts had quit the prison, a carriage whirled up to the prison portals, from which Mrs. Walworth and daughter alighted, and in great haste she said, 'Is my son going to Auburn?' Warden Hubbell replied, 'He has gone.' Hastily regaining their carriage, they were driven rapidly to the depot and arrived there just in time to get on board the train and, with Walworth, take passage to Auburn," stated the *Evening Star* on Dec. 8 1873.

Also aboard the train was a reporter from the *Chicago Daily Tribune*, who spoke with Frank, as the manacled prisoner quietly smoked a cigar under the gaze of prison guards. Along came Ellen, dressed in deep mourning, accompanied by her golden-haired, five-year-old daughter Ruby who asked loudly, "where Mamma was going tonight?" Ellen waved her handkerchief at Frank to get his attention as she arranged for a sleeping car. Frank told the reporter: "I've been well treated at Sing Sing—I can't complain. About going to Auburn, well you know I've got to like it, and there's no good in grumbling. My friends tell me to keep my courage up; I try to. Sometimes

Auburn Prison in New York (1900). New York Digital Heritage.

I hope there is daylight ahead. Perhaps I shall see it before the gray hairs get thick." Then a waiter brought over a chicken lunch Ellen had sent to Frank. "Give my love to my mother, and tell her to keep up her courage and I will mine. Please give my love to my mother. She's a good mother, sir."

Ellen felt responsible for Frank's situation. It is clear her actions demonstrated a single-minded focus to advocate on his behalf. Her home life and the upbringing of her other children were certainly impacted by her devotion to Frank's cause. Her children witnessed the trial, the family sorrows and prisons, which must have been traumatic. Ellen's mother had been an important source of constant support—but that came to an end when Sarah died in bed in July 1874 at age 63 after suffering from a long illness. Her final act to help Ellen was to leave all her property to be divided equally among the grandchildren.

Ellen achieved success in using her connections to improve Frank's living conditions in the prison system. On July 29, 1874—after several months in Auburn Prison—he was moved to a prison asylum for insane convicts. A board of examining physicians determined Frank was epileptic. He would be moved from the prison hospital (where he had been receiving frequent treatments) because the sight of illness and suffering there was becoming a danger to his mind. It was thought he would be better off inside an asylum.

Despite her efforts to obtain a pardon, Ellen was unable to persuade two N.Y. governors to free Frank. She tried with Gov. John Adams Dix, whose two-year term ended December 1874. Efforts continued when Gov. Samuel J. Tilden took office in January 1875. That year, Ellen worked to gain supporters "to pardon her poor Frank" using connections in Washington, D.C., where she had friends. Next she circulated a petition among prominent Kentuckians asking N.Y. Gov. Samuel J. Tilden for a pardon. It didn't work.

Samuel J. Tilden (1814–86). The New York Public Library.

*Transformation: Mrs. Ellen Hardin Walworth not Mrs. Mansfield Tracy*

An important development at this time was Ellen's transformation. She was not a silent victim of domestic violence. Her leadership abilities, sharp intelligence, political acumen and self-sufficiency blossomed as she fought for her eldest son. Ellen was no longer subjugated as before.

The world would benefit from her strength and talents. Among her earliest accomplishments after Manse's death came in 1876 when a need arose to raise funds to renovate Mount Vernon. She was successfully in rallying women and raising money. Speaking of Mount Vernon, Ellen once said that "of all the patriotic impulses and enthusiasms of my life, those connected with Mount Vernon have a peculiarly tender and personal interest; for my own mother, as the first vice-president of the state of New York in

Mount Vernon (1878). Library of Congress.

the Mount Vernon Association, was closely and intimately associated with the earlier efforts and struggles" of the organization. (Formed in 1853 to save the home of George Washington, the association was the first private preservation organization. Its 30 original vice-regents created the first national women's organization in America.)

Also in 1876, Ellen achieved success in collecting exhibits for the Woman's Pavilion in the Centennial

International Exhibition of 1876 in Philadelphia (the first World's Fair held in the United States). During this time she became a member of the Association for the Advancement of Science.

Woman's Pavilion (1876). The New York Public Library.

It is a credit to Ellen's character that she rose so quickly above the terrible public scandal which engulfed her during the murder trial. Despite the widespread sympathy that arose for her with the reading of Manse's horrific letters to her and the details of her family life being known, Ellen must have felt some embarrassment or disgrace—maybe even humiliation. Many women would have sought refuge in hiding, especially in those days when such subjects were taboo (particularly in high society). Ellen, however, held her head high and carried on. Her name began appearing in newspaper articles and on society pages. Rather than simply being known as Mrs. Walworth as before, she was making a name for herself as Mrs. Ellen Hardin Walworth.

She continued to work behind the scenes to secure her son's release from prison. News reports from the summer of 1876 reveal he was suffering from epileptic attacks and becoming dangerously ill in the prison mental hospital. These developments no doubt caused much anguish to Ellen as she lived quietly with her family. A society page noted a visit from her widowed cousin Mrs. Mary Bramlette, the second wife of former Gov. Thomas Elliot Bramlette of Kentucky. During this time that Ellen used her talents to write history that would change the course of her life—propelling her as an author, historian and future founder of the Daughters of the American Revolution. Her entrance came by writing *"The Battle of Saratoga,"* published in 29 pages as the opening article in the May 1877 issue of the scholarly *"Magazine of American History."* Calling it one of the 15 decisive battles in world history, Ellen wrote a stirring account of the 1777 victory for the Continental Army that became a turning point during the second year of the Revolutionary War. "It is a novel thing to find a woman describing [military] campaigns, but Mrs. Walworth accomplishes the work very satisfactorily," declared *The New York Times* on April 22, 1877.

Battle of Saratoga (1858). The New York Public Library.

In fact, three months later the *National Republican* newspaper in Washington, D.C., wrote that Ellen's talented writing on the Battle of Saratoga continued to attract attention. She was able to make her story come alive by including local details because of she had lived in the area for many years.

Another important event followed. Her son—known across the country as Frank Walworth, the parricide—was pardoned in August by incoming N.Y. Gov. Lucius Robinson (1877–79).

"The present mental condition of the prisoner, while it furnishes no ground for his pardon, yet renders the question of his further detention simply one of public morals. Imprisonments done its full work, and the measure of his capability to suffer from it is ended. The only question left is whether the interests of society yet demand the detention of an epileptic in the asylum for insane convicts, where he has so long been placed. ...I can reach no other conclusion than that while upon the evidence given at the trail his conviction was technically proper, he is morally entitled to his release," Robinson noted.

N.Y. Gov. Lucius Robinson. Public domain.

Ellen rushed to join Frank upon his release from prison. She brought with her Tracy, just 9 years old. (Known as a devoted mother, she likely didn't realize the negative toll that the family violence and drama had on Tracy during his formative years. Later in his adult life, Tracy became mentally unstable—unable to complete a medical career or even hold a job, he eventually took his own life at age 59 while living as a recluse in a shack in the woods in Arlington, Va., after repeated suicide attempts. His mental illness surely caused her to suffer also.)

The family left the prison to make their way home by train. A Buffalo newspaper reporter watched as they sat in the Syracuse depot for an hour waiting for a rail connection. "Happily, very few persons knew of their presence, hence they were spared the pain and mortification of being made a public show of it. …A glance at the pale and haggard face of young Walworth is sufficient to convince one that his pardon is an act of the purest humanity if not also of the most exact justice. His hair has grown long since he protracted confinement and he allows it to fall in heavy locks upon his shoulders. He was dressed plainly and spoke but little to his mother, who remained with him and attended to his little wants with untiring devotion."

Headlines in the nation's papers announced the pardon. Many accounts described Frank as looking ill and being "a wreck" since he entered Sing Sing four years earlier. At the Walworth mansion, the family was greeted with congratulatory notes and flowers. News of Frank's return spread through out Saratoga and its hotels. "Long imprisonment and ill health have destroyed the emotional nature of Frank Walworth, and a dull apathy prevents any exhibition of gladness at again being restored to his home and relatives. When taken out for a walk he soon tires and asks to return," noted a columnist from *The Courier-Journal* (Ky.) on Aug. 12, 1877. His quiet and docile demeanor contrasted with Ellen's joy. "There is now such a look of peace upon Mrs. Walworth's face as I never saw before. She called to see me at this hotel last evening. It was the first time she had entered one of the hotels for five years. Her friends feel that she will now be restored to the society she adorns, and from which she has been long missed."

Frank Walworth. Public domain.

And return she did. Several months later, Ellen rose to became president of the Society of Decorative Art of Saratoga. She gave a speech about culture that was reprinted in New York newspapers. A society column in *The Washington Post* in August 1878 remarked that Ellen "has many friends in Washington, who will be glad to hear that she is looking well, and is evidently happier than she has been in many years." Frank began to study law—despite his criminal legal record following his father's and grandfather's career paths.

A year later, Tracy (whose full name was identical to that of his ill-fated father) entered Manse's alma mater Union College in September. An article below by the *Post* provides a revealing glimpse into the family. At that time, Ellen was conducting research to write about the

Mexican-American War in which her father was killed in battle.

## "The Boy Who Killed His Father"

Frank, left, and Tracy Walworth. Public domain.

*"Frank Walworth is here at the old Walworth home, on Broadway. He has not a single feature or trait of character that would indicate that he is a parricide. His health is poor, but he is reading law. He is tall, fair and manly in his bearing, but he has an inexpressibly sad, preoccupied expression. He is, of course, isolated from society. On his exit from prison his former friends cut him, and his proud spirit felt it keenly. His mother has been very busy with her literary work on art and science. She has the respect and sympathy of the entire community here, all of whom are acquainted with the terrible trials she had to endure at the hands of an erratic husband, and her struggles to care for her five children precious to and since his awful death. She is a beautiful woman, on the brink of 50, but, despite her sorrows, she looks 10 years younger. It is presumed the old homestead will be sold, and she will, with this unhappy son, sail for the Old World and join her children now there, hoping to find anchor in some spot where her surroundings will not stir up the unpleasant memories of the past, as they do here."*

Ellen didn't leave for Europe. Instead she continued to expand her professional achievements in Saratoga. This included hosting a keynote event at her home for the local Scientific Association. Her magazine article on the Battle of Buena Vista, which detailed her father's demise, was met with acclaim for its historical detail and descriptiveness.

"The writer reviews briefly the political and military movements which resulted—under such wide and embittered variances of our people in different sections of the country—in opening the war with Mexico, and then gives a vivid and brilliant account of the several engagements which followed," declared the *Boston Evening Transcript* on Dec. 30, 1879. The next year saw her traveling around Kentucky and Illinois to gather information to write about her father's military career.

*Ellen becomes an Advocate for Women*

No longer would Ellen be silent as a victim of domestic violence. She not only became an advocate for herself, but for other women, too. Firmly back in society, she attended a garden party with her children as well as other important public events. Bringing two of her daughters and youngest son, Ellen stayed at Willard's Hotel in Washington, D.C., and rented a house there for a few months to avoid the harsh winter climate of New York. Tracy enrolled in Georgetown College's medical school.

The Walworth mansion became a popular site

for intellectuals. Ellen held evening events devoted to history, poetry and music. She even hosted a Shakespeare symposium and became president of the Saratoga Shakespeare Club. Ellen had a talent for organization and leadership. She was president of the Saratoga Historical Society, a Fellow of the American Geological Society, vice president of the New York State Society of Decorative Art, and a member

Willard Hotel before 1901, when it was torn down and rebuilt. District of Columbia Public Library.

of the New York Genealogical and Biological Society.

Always having to struggle to provide for herself and her children, Ellen rented the mansion during summer vacations as a family hotel. She built a cottage on the grounds for her private use. She listed her occupation in the U.S. census as an author and widow.

In 1880, Ellen was elected as a member of the school board of Saratoga. During her three-year tenure, she championed teaching American history, sanitation standards for students and building a new high school. At the same time, she expanded her interest in science. She wrote an important paper—becoming the first woman to contribute to the Natural History section—for the annual report by The American Association for the Advancement of Science. Her paper was called *"Field Work for Amateurs."* It discussed the importance of involving ordinary women. She declared "that a practical knowledge of natural science will do more for the advancement and emancipation of woman than any laws that can be made, or any rights which can be granted to her." Ellen encouraged professional male scientists to invite women to participate in science.

As Ellen's literary and public-service career took off, her children began to leave the nest. She had become a trustee on the Saratoga Monument Association, the only group of its kind to have a woman hold this important post.

In 1881, Frank became an attorney and was admitted to the bar in Ithaca, N.Y. His life was out of the public eye. He took up an interest in archery and rose quickly due to his talent. A rare news article revealed him leading an archery meeting. His skills were mentioned frequently in *The Bicycling World & Archery Field* magazine. It published his writings and poetry. One indication of his gift for shooting a bow and arrows was a championship match he won in Brooklyn that year. Among a group of six competitors, he scored the most hits and points by shooting at distances of 60, 80 and 100 yards. He also was mentioned often as the archery partner of Corinne Bramlette, stepdaughter of his mother's Kentucky cousin.

Soon afterwards, poor health was cited as a reason for his brief move to Texas. A couple of years later he returned to New York. In December 1883, he and Corinne married. Ellen held a small wedding reception at the Walworth mansion attended by immediate family and friends.

That month, Clara, age 12, entered the Convent of the Sacred Heart. She made her final vows as a nun nearly two years later, receiving the cross from her uncle Father Clarence. An odd incident about Clara is contained in a family genealogy book. She was living in a convent school in Boston where she taught art. One summer night she was recovering from an illness in her room when a fire broke out on the convent's roof near the cupola. She had been resting inside after being ordered to stay there quietly until further notice. The convent and school had been undergoing construction before the blaze began after 8 p.m. According to news accounts, tongues of fire danced around a gold cross there as the inferno spread. Within 15 minutes, flames leapt from the upper windows. As other nuns rushed past her door carrying buckets of water, Clara remained silently seated on her chair without moving. Rather than join the nuns to battle the blaze, save students or flee, Clara just stayed quietly in her room. It is extraordinary she didn't behave as most people would in that situation. Instead she remained in her position until ordered by her religious superior to leave. Then she joined 250 nuns who fled from the burning building to safety. Her behavior could be due to religious obedience taken to an extreme level, or it may be she was afraid to disobey an order due to the abusive environment that her controlling father created in her childhood. Whatever the case, Clara and her family members were never far from tragedy.

While Clara remained in Boston, Ellen's passion for history led to another important role. She joined a board of trustees for the Historical Society of Saratoga. Its objective was to collect relics of the early residents of northern New York. Through her efforts, 17 memorial tables were placed to mark historic spots in the Battle of Saratoga. She was also active in the Saratoga Monument Association.

Always the devoted mother, Ellen briefly moved with Tracy to Florida during 1885. The warmer weather was meant to help Tracy recover from an attack of typhoid fever. His deteriorating health was partly attributed to the stress he suffered during his medical studies in college. Three years earlier, he had helped with arrangements for graduation exercises at Georgetown College's medical department. After feeling better, Tracy and his sister Nellie sailed to Europe for a few months rest.

A fatal illness next befell the family. On Oct. 29, 1886, Frank died suddenly at age 33 from bronchitis at the family home. His daughter was only eight months old. Unable to practice law for a couple of years due to bad health, he had been confined to the house for three weeks before his passing. Frank had been in charge of the math department in the school that Ellen had started. "Both his mother and wife, with his brother and sisters, who comprise the household are prostrated with grief and will have the sympathy of many friends," noted *The New York Times*. Frank's young wife never remarried. She stayed in the mansion and raised her daughter there.

A small funeral was held for Frank on Nov. 3, 1886. Family members attended the 11 a.m. service at the family home. Despite strong Catholicism practiced by Ellen's children and uncle Father Clarence, the funeral service was conducted by Protestant clergy. Local press reports didn't Father Clarence. Instead it was officiated by Frank's cousin Presbyterian Rev. Clarence W. Backus, of Victor, N.Y., assisted by Episcopal Rev. Dr. Joseph Carey and Presbyterian Rev. C.J. Young.

---

**DEATH OF FRANK M. WALWORTH.**

**The Last of a Principal Actor in a Celebrated Murder-Case Thirteen Years Ago.**

SARATOGA, Oct. 30.—Frank H. Walworth, who killed his father, Mansfield Walworth, at the Sturtevant House, New York city, June 2, 1873, died yesterday at his home in this city, of pneumonia, at the age of thirty-one. He leaves a wife, the daughter of the late Governor Bramlette, of Kentucky, and one child. He was a grandson of Chancellor Reuben H. Walworth, a noted lawyer of the State, and his maternal grandfather was Col. J. J. Hardin, of Illinois, who was killed at Buena Vista.

Frank Walworth's murder of his father created a great sensation at the time. He was impelled to the deed by the fact that his father, from whom his mother had obtained a divorce on the ground of cruel treatment, persistently annoyed the family by writing letters threatening Mrs. Walworth and blackening her character. Frank had warned him in vain to desist, and finally, after a stormy interview, shot and killed him. Young Walworth was defended by Charles O'Conor, but was convicted of murder in the second degree. He was sentenced to State prison for life, but was pardoned by Governor Robinson in 1877. He was admitted to the bar in 1881.

*The Indianapolis Journal*, Oct. 31, 1886.

220

Burial followed in Greenridge Cemetery at the Walworth plot, also the final resting place of his father.

Ellen's activities after Frank's death a slowed down during a time of mourning. Her health was affected, and she no longer participated in the school. Nelly managed the school and taught there. (Later, Nelly moved to Albany to teach.)

Instead, Ellen occupied herself with her busy schedule, while her children became involved in their own pursuits. Her youngest surviving daughter, fair-haired Ruby, was enrolled in Vassar College, where in 1888 she was winning tennis tournaments. Nelly was busy writing a book— *"The Life and Times of Kateri Tekakwitha: The Lily of the Mohawks 1656–1680"*—about a Catholic convert that would be published in 1893. During the cold New England winters, Ellen traveled to milder climates because her health had become more frail.

THE LIFE AND TIMES

OF

KATERI TEKAKWITHA

The Lily of the Mohawks.

1656–1680.

BY

ELLEN H. WALWORTH,
AUTHOR OF "AN OLD WORLD, AS SEEN THROUGH YOUNG EYES."

Books by Ellen's daughter and namesake.

AN OLD WORLD,

OR

SEEN THROUGH YOUNG EYES:

OR,

TRAVELS AROUND THE WORLD.

BY

ELLEN H. WALWORTH.

"How beautiful the world is! and how wide!"—LONGFELLOW.

It is also noteworthy that in 1888 two of Manse's books were published posthumously: *"Married in Mask"* (with the veiled references to Ellen which had been serialized) was published as a complete novel by A.L. Burt of N.Y. and *"Zahara,*

*A Leaf for the Empire"* (which told of the discovery of an uninhabited North Pole city where an ancient civilization lived) published by G.W. Dillingham, also of N.Y. A commentary in *The Critic* magazine on Nov. 10, 1888 referred to *"Zahara* as " written in the Land of the Shades" because it was published 15 years after Manse's death. "There is something appropriately 'shady,' but the way, about the publication of a dead man's manuscript as 'A New Novel,' without note or comment, so long after he has joined the majority," it declared. If any royalties were earned from the publication of these books, the funds likely went to Ellen's children. Manse would have been paid for the earlier work that was serialized before he died. But this printing was a first for *"Zahara."*

Given that both books were issued in the same year, it would seem that Manse's heirs (children) would have been behind this effort and probably needed the cash. If this was the case, Ellen would have known and likely helped her children. It may even have been her idea as a way to obtain funds since she always struggled with financial difficulties.

No society columns featured Ellen's comings and goings, nor events at her home for several years after Frank's death. In fact, there is little mention of her activities at all. She became a trustee of the Board of Education in Saratoga and a life member of the American Historical Association.

Money troubles in 1890 again forced Ellen to move permanently to Washington, D.C.—as was the case with all of the four founders of DAR. Respectable women—unmarried and widowed—found decent paying jobs with good hours as government clerks. Her connections enabled her to obtain a position at the U.S. Census Office, not a permanent office but an impromptu branch of the Interior Department. Prior to taking a job there, new applicants had to pass an exam given by a former schoolmaster Prof. James H. Blodgett, Census editor—26% of the 1,968 applicants failed, according to the *Evening Star* on Aug. 16, 1890. Obviously Ellen had no problem passing the test despite her lack of a formal education. She joined 110,000 people employed in the civil service scattered among various departments.

It was a busy time when she took up her post. She worked among 2,000 clerks in the D.C. offices as they prepared to administer the next U.S. Census, which began in June 1890. The Census Office had been recruiting staff, including enumerators, a year in advance. Newspapers across the country told of this project. "The 11th Census will be counted by the aid of electricity," marveled a writer for "the *Fort Worth Daily Gazette* in May 1890. "At first this seems rather a startling statement, but if any of my readers would only come to the Census Office and see the electrical counting and sorting machines now at work on some of the special data, the thing would be made clear to them at once."

Ellen took an apartment in the swank Langham Hotel, on the corner of 14th and H streets N.W.

Diplomats, lawmakers and the city's social set held many events there. In this thriving city, she moved in literary circles with like-minded, independent women who shared a passion for American history. She even had one of her poems published in the *Washington Post.*

With Ellen's participation, the Daughters of the American Revolution became an actual organization during a meeting attended by Mary Desha and Eugenia Washington. Only those three founders were present at that notable event due to storm that swept over the city that night, plus the fact that many other interested women were away during DC's sweltering summer months. "Brilliant, witty, gifted with charm and personality as well as beauty, she always rallied about her a spirited following, and reigned supreme among her young and old friends

Rare image of the Langham Hotel where Ellen lived. A preliminary meeting about starting DAR was held in her apartment Aug. 9, 1890. This drawing was done that year. *"Illustrated Washington, Our Capitol"* by American Publishing and Engraving (1890).

wherever she was," recalled Ella Loraine Dorsey of DAR, in August 1915.

Ellen was assigned DAR's National Number 5. From then on, Ellen championed DAR and worked tirelessly to promote patriots and history. She was the first editor of the society's *American Monthly Magazine* in 1892 and served for two years. She chaired the press and publications committee at DAR's first Continental Congress in 1892. Ellen also became the first recording secretary general and in 1894 was made honorary vice-president general. She

### GARLANDS FOR OUR HEROES.

O peaceful army! move with quiet tread,
  And bear the trophies, of victorious spring.
Go! lay them at the feet of heroes, dead,
  While to their deeds fond memories backward wing.

Heroic deeds that stir our hearts with pride,
  While dwelling on the glories round us spread,
Cemented with the blood whose lavish tide
  Flowed from the wounds of these, our sacred dead,

Bring garlands for our heroes! forest buds
  We've fondly gathered near stern rocks and snows;
Whose dainty odors lived 'mid surging floods,
  As tenderness in bravest hearts o'er glows.

Bring garlands for our heroes! lilies white,
  Whose golden tongues may toll a gentle knell,
Heartsense for calmness, while our souls invite
  Sad visions of the fields on which they fell.

Bring garlands for our heroes! roses red,
  And roses white, as orphaned children's prayers,
Or blushing buds for boyish souls that fled
  Amid the carnage where they knew no fears.

Bring all your rarest flowers, and weave them well,
  Or fling them broadcast o'er the modest graves
That hold unwritten histories 'neath their swell,
  Like hidden treasures under ocean waves.

Bring heavy garlands for the great, the wise!
  Whose broad expanse of mind—whose firm decrees
Could sweep the horizon of a nation's skies,
  And guide its shattered bark o'er stormy seas.
            ELLEN HARDIN WALWORTH.
  WASHINGTON, Decoration Day, 1890.

Ellen's patriotic poem she wrote for Memorial Day (then called Decoration Day), *Washington Post*, May 30, 1890.

was among a group of notable women who attended a reception of White House cabinet officers. Ellen became a member of a DAR chapter organized in 1894 in Saratoga Springs and remained a member there for the rest of her life.

"It was Mrs. Walworth who suggested the idea of having the portrait of the first President General, Mrs. Benjamin Harrison, painted by Daniel Huntington, and placed in the White House. Her efforts in this direction were successful, and at the Continental Congress in 1894, the picture of Caroline Scott Harrison was presented to the Executive Mansion, where it now hangs," according to a DAR article.

DAR painting of First Lady Caroline Scott Harrison (1832–1892) by Daniel Huntington, a prominent painter in the New York art world. Image courtesy of DAR.

Life in the nation's capital was exciting for Ellen. She took advantage of numerous opportunities to showcase her talents. She read an extract of her work on the Battles of Saratoga during an event with Sen. Joseph Roswell Hawley from Connecticut. Reubena (Ruby) paused her studies at Vassar to move in with her mother in D.C., where she obtained a job in the Patent Office. Society articles frequently mentioned their names attending events together. One was a tea before the society entrance for the daughter of architect Lewis Morris Hallowell. But the high life would come to an end.

Ellen went back to New York accompanied by Ruby, who resigned from the Patent Office in April 1892. Ellen lost her job at the Census Office, which became embroiled in a scandal related to mismanagement and waste. Apparently, she had overseen the work of at least 50 clerks tasked for 10 months with gathering financial statistics on schools. An investigation of the Census Office found that taxpayer funds for $35,0000 worth of material collected under Ellen's supervision was thrown away as worthless. It is remains unknown whose idea it was to pursue this line of inquiry for nearly a year only to destroy materials prepared and printed. Some of the blame for the waste of public money fell on statistical chief T. Campbell Copeland, a former English Army officer, for being a foreigner unfamiliar with American needs, according to *The New York Times* in May 1892.

Ellen continued to soar despite bureaucratic controversy. She busied herself with patriotic activities with DAR and Saratoga in New York. An address she gave in July 1893 at the World's Fair in Chicago on the *"Value of National Archives"* became instrumental in launching the U.S. National Archives.

With a strong track record for writing historic articles, she became a trustee of the American Authors' Guild in 1894. The goal

World's Fair in Chicago in 1892. Library of Congress.

of the organization was to protect the literary business interests of writers. Another example of her leadership and strong intellect is a discussion she held at the group the following year on international copyright law, piracy issues and the need to reduce the postal rates on manuscripts to be the same as for newspapers.

No one would ever guess she had once been subjugated and living under the cloud of Manse's decades of abuse. Ellen's sense of public service and use of her talents to preserve history had a positive impact everywhere she went. Back in Saratoga, she made an important address on history in the opera house during a local celebration. The town had gathered for a grand parade of 60 carriages and floats, along with a floral evening ball. Ellen's role of honor demonstrates how well regarded she was by those in her community. She also found time to lead a committee of the Saratoga Monument Association, reporting that 3,000 people had visited the site in a year and $5,000 had been earned in August 1891. The next spring found Ellen visiting her brother Gen. Martin Harding at his Spanish-style home in St. Augustine, Fla. There he gave a dance reception for Ellen's daughter Ruby and her cousin Evelyn (Lem's daughter).

During this period, Ruby returned to her studies at Vassar. Her personality and interests seemed to be much like her vivacious mother. Ruby was interested in the arts, writing, volunteering, DAR and history.

She also had a passion for poetry. She had written a comic poem published in 1888 called *"Where was Elsie? Or the Saratoga Fairies."* Like her brother Frank, who had his poetry published in the archery magazine, Ruby also contributed her poems to periodicals. By the time Ruby graduated from Vassar in 1896 with a diploma in painting, she had already been the class poet and former art editor of *The Vassarian.* One of Ruby's poems published at Vassar is below.

Gen. Martin Hardin, possibly Lem's daughter center, and Ruby Walworth, right. Library of Congress.

### Attainment

*We seek through desert wastes in vain*
*Where living waters lie,*

*We struggle on through toil and pain*
*To find the spring is dry.*

*But when despair would drag us down,*
*And hope inspires no more,*

*A sense seems born our work to crown —*
*We hear the torrent's roar.*

—*R.H. Walworth '96*

Ellen continued to edit DAR's magazine, while promoting both this growing patriot organization and American history.

Ellen and Ruby maintained their close relationship. In 1894, they both supported the annual meeting in New York of the Vassar Students' Aid Society, formed to raise funds and loan money to students. The two women continued to be active in this group. Ellen also participated in a New York City meeting of the Woman's Christian Temperance Union to protest selling alcohol on Sundays. The group signed a petition to the state legislature. "We, the undersigned, believing in the sanctity of the Sabbath, and seeing in the coming effort to open the salons on the Lord's day a menace to good morals, good government, and to the safety and happiness of the home, earnestly protest against such action on the part of the Legislature, and request you, our representative in the Assembly, to vote against it." Ellen's opposition may have been rooted in her experiences with Manse, who had been described as violent when drunk.

She spent a good deal of time in New York City doing various activities in 1895. There she participated in regular monthly meetings of the American Authors' Guild. She was also began attending the Woman's Law Class of New York University. Her interest was in parliamentary law.

Ellen also attended the first annual convention of the State Federation of Women's Clubs and Societies. She was nominated as president of the group. "The election was a most exciting one. This was partially due to a strong feeling in regard to the candidates and partly, as has been said, to the knowledge of parliamentary law which the New York City women have been absorbing during the last year," stated *The New York Times* in November 1895. Another newspaper described the election, saying Ellen "is credited with being a clever woman, but she is not generally known." This may explain why Ellen lost the election with only 45 votes compared to the winning ballot of 65. Undeterred by the loss, Ellen lent

Hotel Majestic at Central Park in 1895. Library of Congress.

her voice wherever it was needed. She gave a lecture on "Parliamentary Practices" to a woman's group at the Hotel Majestic a month later. The event was carried in the major NYC newspapers.

The following year Ruby also obtained an artist's studio in the city. Ellen remained a visible mover and shaker among women there. She attended a tea for Vassar Student's Aid Society. At an annual luncheon of the Brooklyn's Woman's Club, Ellen "spoke of the despotism which formerly gave the direction and management of women's clubs to a few women, and the change for the better in this respect." This mention in the local *Times Union* newspaper shows Ellen's use of her legal knowledge to improve the composition of women's clubs from elitism to be more welcoming to different types of women.

MRS. ELLEN HARDIN WALWORTH.

Autographed drawing of Ellen as a legal scholar (1898). Library of Congress.

Ellen's next career milestone is yet another example of her courage, determination and brilliance. At age 63 she became a law graduate from New York University. She was among 47 women awarded diplomas. During the ceremony in April 1896 held in the concert hall of Madison Square Garden, Ellen read an essay and won a prize for scholarship. Her topic was *"Do Legislatures Make Laws?"* This was an important even for women's rights since women were prohibited from practicing law at the time. Ellen made the most of her newfound legal knowledge.

A few months after graduating, she became a university extension lecturer in a small branch of the Albany State Library. Every Thursday she was on hand with law books. Later she founded the Post Parliament, New York to promote the study and practice of parliamentary law as well as the study of legislative and executive branches of government. The group boasted 125 members who regularly held debates and a moot parliament on different phases of legislation. Ellen also encouraged business training for women. She also gave lectures on law enforcement and incorporations. Newspapers are filled with notices of her talks to women's groups on parliamentary law. "Women lack a knowledge of this method of rule. They have been laughed at by husbands, brothers and friends until they have been goaded to *'Cushing's Manual [of Rules of Proceeding and Debate in Deliberative Assemblies]'* in self-defense," noted *The Buffalo Enquirer* in October 1896, after mentioning a talk by Ellen.

A month later, she even taught a five-lesson course on parliamentary practice in organizations and the science of government to women in Yonkers. She charged $5 per course, which were limited to 20 students. One class was devoted to different forms of organization, with another on the procedure of motions. Classes were even held in Ruby's Midtown Manhattan apartment and art studio at 152 West 57th St. (today the location of the Carnegie Hall Tower). Ruby had been studying art in the city after graduating from Vassar and found a teaching job at The Misses Ely's School for Girls for heiresses and daughters of millionaires. Founded by three suffragettes, the elite boarding school was located on Riverside Drive near 85th and 86th streets. During the summer she taught art classes outdoors in Saratoga to earn extra income to help support her mother.

"The most important study for the women of today is the science of government. Unless women understand this, how can they know whether their officers are competent or not. Besides, discontent may arise from an unparliamentary way of putting things, or by silence an affirmative vote may be given, although the women may be just boiling over with rage. Debate is a species of social athletics most useful to women," Ellen told the Fort Greene DAR Chapter in 1897. She wore her collegiate cap and gown while presenting a six-part course to the group.

Some accounts of Ellen's life mistakenly say that her successful efforts to obtain a pardon for Frank were due to her education in law. This is incorrect because she formally studied law many years later. Her father, who took charge of her early education, was a lawyer in Illinois. Her brother Lem and son Frank also were attorneys, as were the Chancellor and Frank. It should be remembered also that her emphasis in law was to empower women in civil and legislative matters rather than in criminal courts. She urged coeducation in the study of government as well as the need for school children to learn about the U.S. Constitution. Ellen sought to use law to change society as well as to include and empower women to govern. Her father had been a prosecutor, but later served in the state legislature and Congress. He likely was her role model.

During this time in her life, Ellen lived in New York City but still maintained her ties to Saratoga where she reigned during a summer jubilee week. She spoke on *"Municipal Reform and the Civic Club of Philadelphia"* and arranged celebrations for the 4th of July. She was featured prominently in an article on a state meeting of women in Saratoga titled *"Brilliant Women as Guests"* in *The Buffalo Enquirer* on July 8, 1896. It mentioned Ellen as a being among a "conclave of intellect" in splendid gowns "whom Saratoga delights to honor." There she gave a talk called "Art and Science in Summer Clouds." She closed out the year with attending the opening session of the 12th annual meeting of the American Historical Association in Columbia University. There she rubbed shoulders with a crowd of mostly male academics from leading institutions in the United States, including future president Woodrow Wilson, then a Princeton professor.

Men look at a broken bike on a path (1897). Library of Congress.

As President of the Woman's Association for Greater Saratoga, Ellen led a drive in 1897 that raised $70 for bicycle paths. It boasted 1,600 members, who could join for 10 cents a year. A major objective of the group was to enlist the state of New York to buy the 50 springs in the area for the public.

The clash of war drums sounded in the spring of

1898. Cuba had been struggling to gain independence from Spain since February. Newspapers engaged in yellow journalism by sensationalizing news rather than presenting facts to garner sympathy for Cuba. Congress passed resolutions supporting Cuba as the U.S. prepared for war with Spain. With war inevitable

MRS. ELLEN HARDIN WALWORTH

*Chicago Tribune, 1895.*

(even though Spain didn't declare war on the U.S. until April 24), Ellen's sense of patriotism stirred. She led a nationwide call for women volunteers from her residence in a four-story brick house in New York City's Upper West Side at 251 West 88th St. Her letter was published April 2 in newspapers across the nation.

> *"In view of the crisis through which our country is now passing and of the imminent presence of war, it is fitting that the patriotic women of the country should prepare, as our government is preparing, for the possibility of war. While our desire is for peace ... our nation teaches us that peace is often gained and maintained by the skill and strength that prepare for war. As patriotic women our duties are distinct and clear in the event of war, for again history enforces the fact that in every war through which our nation has passed on to victory, the efforts, the sacrifices and prayers of women have been efficient aids to the attainment of such victories.*

*"The honor of our country and the suffering of men, women and children in the Island of Cuba 'for the cause of independence' call for an early and earnest enlistment of women in a suitable service for our country. I therefore call for volunteers in sanitary, medical and other ways suitable for women and for auxiliary volunteers to aid and encourage the active workers. The value of organization is unquestioned, and by means of these two cooperative bodies many women will be ready to do something in the hour or need. Prudence and conservatism are necessarily elements of well directed action; therefore the following limitations are made:*

*"Every active sanitary volunteer shall be not less than 25 years of age; if a married woman she must be without young children or other home duties requiring her constant personal attention. While it is not supposed that such volunteers will be called from their homes, there may be occasions which demand united action or deliberation at one or more points.*

*"A corps of auxiliary volunteers will also be enlisted who shall be ready for aid and forward the work of the active volunteers; the auxiliaries may include women of all ages and condition and also patriotic children.*

*"I pledge myself to active work, and shall be pleased to receive the names and addresses of women who are willing to enlist active volunteers and auxiliary volunteers and shall begin to organize at once on the following plan, approved by committees in Washington and New York City..."*

Within two weeks, she reported that more than 50 women had volunteered as nurses. She then coordinated a group of doctors to provide them with medical training. Ellen's sharp intellect was revealed in an interview published April 17, 1898 by *The Los Angeles Times.* She surmised that a war would likely be fought near Cuba under hot tropical conditions that would result in yellow fever. She wanted to prepare to treat the wounded in such an environment. She thought it would be good to train volunteer nurses to care for disabled soldiers and assist in surgeries. Ellen also considered collecting donations for a hospital ship and ambulances.

She also spoke about how DAR could support this effort. "I have already had letters from daughters who are eager and anxious to take part, if need be. A rich western girl writes that she is prepared to donate her money, time and strength. Another announces that she will do anything—even to carrying arms. My own daughter [Ruby, age 30] is ready to do anything required of her, without a moment's warning, whether to nurse in a hospital, give out supplies or go to the front with orders. I pledge myself to active work, and shall be glad to encourage other daughters to do the same."

The following month Ellen helped found the Woman's National War Relief Association of the USA, incorporated in Albany. Its members included Mrs. Ulysses S. Grant, Mrs. Roger Wolcott (wife of the governor of Massachusetts) and Mrs. Mary Harrison

McKee, daughter of former president Benjamin Harrison. The group donated funds to the Surgeon General's Army and Navy fund and helped to equip two

U.S.S. *Solace* hospital ship (1898). Library of Congress.

hospital ships—the U.S.S. *Relief* in New York harbor and the U.S.S. *Solace* in the Brooklyn Navy Yard—to accompany troop ships to Cuba.

The women raised $3,000 in the organization's first week. "One of our chief aims is to preserve the health of our soldiers and sailors. We believe that this is the most efficient way to help their families. If the families need relief there are many organizations to provide it; let them do it. We are working for war. We are working for victory. To gain this we want to put our men in the best possible condition," Ellen said.

When you read her statements you can't help but recall that her father died so far away from home while at war with Mexico. She had studied and written about his death in battle. This knowledge and her sufferings regarding his ultimate sacrifice surely played a part in her determined mission to care for soldiers. It seems that her desires stemmed from both patriotism and her personal experiences to help spare other families from what happened to the Hardins, including her brother Martin.

Not only were Ellen and the other women concerned about supplying medical goods and nurses to care for the sick and wounded, but they also wanted the men to have the best external surroundings. Donations were being collected to paint the *Relief* with green linings for the awnings. "This color will prove grateful to the eyes of convalescent soldiers lounging on deck," reported *The New York Times* on June 14, 1898. That same newspaper called Ellen one of the hardest workers in the group. She regularly conducted inspections of field as well as regimental and division hospitals to see what supplies were needed and determine how to improve conditions.

She also made arrangements for Otis Elevator Co. to install an elevator inside the *Relief*. The vessel was a coastal passenger steamship bought by the Army and transformed into the most modern floating hospitals of its time with electric fans. It had two large medical wards on each deck and 300 beds, plus room for 200 beds on the upper deck under the canvas awnings. It also had isolation wards for contagious diseases and a life-saving x-ray machine donated by General Electric. Volunteers equipped the ship with one of the latest scientific innovations—an apparatus to prepare carbonated bottled water. Her group spent $3,600 that month on fittings for the *Relief* and *Solace* and supplies for the front.

Without regard for her well-being, she also visited the U.S. General Hospital in Fort Myer, Va., that had 400 patients. The Army sent men there who were suffering from pneumonia, typhoid fever and meningitis.

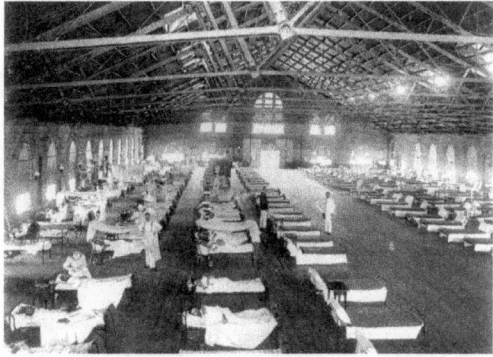

Dining hall in Fort Meyer used as a hospital (1898). Library of Congress.

Ellen carried a letter to give her admittance to all military hospitals. In July she visited the hospital in Fort Monroe, Va., with its 440 patients were being transported there from Cuba. "One would imagine that it would be a distressing and harrowing scene to take a stroll through the wards of the hospital or drive the long line of hospital tents, but it is not. The fumes of iodoform fill the air, but there are only exceptional cases where a man is found who shows signs of physical suffering. They are the most cheerful lot, these wounded soldiers, that could be found in a day's journey. Some men have lost a leg, some an arm, and others have been shot in different parts of the body, but they are all smiling, and never a whimper is heard," noted *The New York Times* on July 24, 1898. "Every patient is provided with a suit of pajamas, and many of the invalids have now improved so rapidly that they are permitted to go out daily for a walk. It is a ludicrous scene, and yet it is pathetic to see the poor fellows hobbling down the main street of Fort

Monroe in their gayly colored pajamas." In a letter to the Association during one visit there, she wrote: "This morning I was

Tents at Fort Monroe (1898). Indiana State Library.

talking with a surgeon, who said an officer was unable to start home, because he could not go away without crutches. The government does not allow them to take crutches away, nor are they allowed to buy any. Luckily, just as I was having this conversation, an expressman came up with an extra pair of crutches you had sent. I turned them over to the officer, and he was able to leave for home today." After leaving Fort Monroe, Ellen had 50 pairs of crutches sent there immediately.

Ellen also traveled to Camp Thomas in Chickamauga Park, Ga., which was an assembly point for cavalry regiments going to Tampa, Fla. She also organized military quarters for eight trained nurses. The group also donated 600 abdominal bandages and 12 dozen cans each of condensed milk and beef extract. The women also accepted a San Diego man's offer to donate a carload of lemons, which were distributed in New York City.

The women helped in every conceivable way. Some even became hospital cooks. Women also sewed clothing for the injured. Ellen's association even sent a French chef to Fort Monroe to cook for wounded soldiers there after she

Nurses quarters at U.S. Army Sternberg General Hospital at Camp Thomas (1898). National Library of Medicine.

thought the food was unsuitable for the sick. Some $1,000 was raised to cover the costs of installing electric stoves on the *Missouri* hospital ship. Other donations made it possible to send six portable oil stoves to a doctor in Jacksonville, Fla., to help cook food for ill soldiers. "Owing to the over-taxing for government nurses, she [Mrs. Ellen Hardin Walworth] offered to pay half the cost of eight nurses. This offer was accepted and the nurses have been stationed at the fort," the *Times* noted in July.

Ellen's organization also worked to have wooden planks placed under tents at Camp Wikoff on Montauk Point in Long Island. Its hospital was a covered passageway over 16 rows of tents containing 500 cots. Ellen helped fill one request at Camp Wikoff to provide the hospital with shirts and pajamas for the men as well as Lithia water for fever patients. Other shipments there included a truck load of fruit, 200 pajamas, 150 suits of underclothing, slippers,

Ill soldiers waiting in New York to be transported from a hospital ship to Camp Wikoff (Sept. 10, 1898). National Library of Medicine.

books and magazines.

Ellen frequently traveled to provide help at Fort Monroe, where Ruby worked as a nurse. The fort provided Ruby with a comfortable and sheltered environment in which she treated the sick and injured. She was determined to do her part in the war effort and took a brief nursing training course at Saratoga Hospital. Putting her career as an artist and teacher on hold, Ruby had declared, "If I cannot fight, I can nurse." Her first assignment was at Fort Monroe where she took charge of two sets of patients due to a shortage of nurses.

In August, Ellen moved to Camp Wikoff to remain as long as needed. The camp had been hastily set up that month at Montauk Point on Long Island as an open-air quarantine site to contain any diseases brought by returning soldiers (to prevent the spread to hospitals or the public). When cleared, soldiers could be released. The camp had two areas each with a hospital: a quarantined Detention Hospital area and a General Hospital for

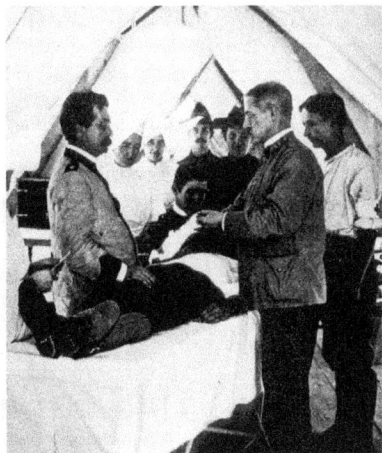

Operating table in the General Hospital field surgical ward at Camp Wikoff (Sept. 17, 1898). National Library of Medicine.

the larger population of weakened and recovering men. Ellen lived in a tent in the general area. She was so loved by the soldiers that they called her the camp's mother, according to newspaper report in August. "Mrs. Walworth has been untiring in her efforts for the soldiers. She has been alert in their interest, and often the prompt arrival of supplies has been due solely to her. On one occasion she drove 20 miles to get them milk, and she remains on the spot to see that the soldiers lack nothing."

Soon after Ellen arrived, Ruby joined her as a volunteer nurse—placing herself in more danger due to the illnesses there. Both mother and daughter were there to greet the arrival of the first troops with 500 sandwiches they had prepared. Ruby helped Ellen order and organize medical supplies. Sisters of Charity nurses worked at the General Hospital.

Ellen later wrote, "In the midst of these busy, useful days, she [Ruby] heard the surgeon from the Detention Hospital, at the dispensary, asking for supplies and help. She heard him say he had no woman nurse, nor scarcely a male nurse who was competent.

245

Red Cross nurse fans sick soldier on a stretcher at railroad station at Camp Wikoff (Sept. 17, 1898). National Library of Medicine.

Immediately she offered her services. She then came to my tent and assisted me in preparing two wagon loads of supplies for the Detention Hospital, and then said, 'Mother, in 15 minutes I shall have my trunk packed and everything ready to go there as a nurse. I want you to take me there, and let it be seen that I have a protector at call; and then you know, mother, you cannot come again.' It is needless to say that I set before her the risk she ran, and the good work she was doing at the General Hospital. Her firm but gentle reply was, 'Yes, mother, but there are plenty of people here to help you. There, at the Detention Hospital, is the real need; that is the place for me. It is what I intend to do.'"

Ruby had volunteered at the dreaded Detention Hospital because no other woman would. She took charge of the Contagion Ward and ordered from Ellen large quantities of food, medical supplies, Lithia water to the Detention Hospital and the Contagion Ward. "She wrote a hurried note to me every day, and pinned it on her tent, for my messenger to bring, telling me how she was and what were the needs of her patients and others in the hospitals," stated Ellen. "Her success in bringing patients safely through the disease of diphtheria, measles and malignant malarial or suspected yellow fever attest her skill and devotion as a nurse, as do the touching letters from several of those to whom she ministered."

While treating the suffering at Camp Wikoff, Ruby penned this poem. Several days later it was printed in newspapers in New York and Washington, D.C.

*Written Sept. 3, Montauk, N.Y.*
*Detention Hospital at Camp Wikoff*

*The ocean moans low where the death rattle shakes,*
*The wind howls a dirge o'er the desolate lakes;*

*We're burying our boys whom the cannon passed by,*
*Whom care might have saved, we have brought home*
*to die.*

*We're burying the victors who trampled on Spain,*
*On Nation, awake! Right the wrong, fix the blame.*

*Cry "Shame!" for starvation, cry "Shame!"*
*for neglect;*
*Let justice be done, let the blows be direct.*

*The wind howls a dirge o'er the victors of Spain;*
*Oh Nation, awake! Right the wrong, fix the blame!*
*—Reubena Hyde Walworth*

Typhoid fever was rampant. On Sept. 7, 1898, *The New York Times* described about 20 soldiers stricken with fever taken from Camp Wikoff in need of treatment in a Tarrytown hospital. A

Secretary of War reviews troops at Camp Wikoff (1898). National Archives and Records Administration.

committee was sent to look for accommodations and volunteer doctors. It was during this time of great illness at the camp that Ruby continued to work tirelessly.

"For many weeks she was the only woman in this infected camp, pitched upon a hill fronting the limitless horizon of the Atlantic, restless waters and silently passing ships on one hand, and on the other the equally silent cemetery, where day by day melancholy processions came and went. Holding no communication with the outside world, isolated because of the infection, she there passed weeks of trying labor, but of happiness, the lofty aspirations of her idealistic nature satisfied in complete forgetfulness of self," according to a *Women's National War Relief Association Report* published in 1899.

A week after writing her sad poem, Ruby became ill. She refused to leave her post until the last patient was discharged and the Detention Hospital closed. Only then did she go to her mother's tent in the camp.

On Sept. 29, the *Times* ran an article about Ruby called *"Volunteer Nurse Has Fever."* It noted she was the only hospital nurse from the Women's National War Relief Association to go to Montauk Point. It said she returned to the city 10 days earlier feeling sick, was admitted to Presbyterian Hospital and diagnosed with typhoid fever. Ruby lingered for five weeks until she died at the hospital. It must have been extremely difficult for Ellen to know that Ruby died Oct. 18 without her present since no visitors had been allowed due to the fear of contagion.

"Miss Walworth's splendid service deserves the gratitude of every American. It was as important as the work of soldiers on the battlefields. She was a heroine of the purest and noblest kind. Many a man has she nursed back to life and health. Her constancy and skill were such that she never lost a case. She furnishes a shining example among women of heroic and patriotic self-sacrifice," noted *The Standard Union* (Brooklyn) newspaper on Oct. 19, 1898.

The next day, the *Times* printed the following poem by Charles Hanson Towne under her name.

# Reubena    Hyde
## Walworth

*No storm of praise will*
*be bestowed on her,*
*Sweet nurse—yea,*
*angel-gentle minister,*
*And yet she served her*
*flag—not as a man,*
*But better still, as only*
*woman can.*

Reubena (Ruby) Hyde Walworth, also a DAR member and page. The Saratoga Springs History Museum.

Public praise was bestowed upon Ruby far and wide. "Her mother has many old friends in Louisville, who knew the brave girl when a child that sympathize with her in her great loss," *The Courier-Journal* stated a week after Ruby's death.

Ruby was buried Greenridge Cemetery in Saratoga Springs with full military honors by some of the veterans she served. On the one-year anniversary of her death, members of DAR's Saratoga chapter erected a 41-foot granite monument to Ruby in a special dedication ceremony. The *Evening Star* wrote that Ruby's death was "proof that the women of our land are loyal to their country and to humanity, even to the point of laying down their lives, and the power of our society is manifested in the life and death of this one daughter."

Two months before the war ended in December 1898, the federal government began an investigation of Camp Wikoff. A 21-page document detailed poor conditions there. It stated that when the first troops (275 men) arrived at the camp on Aug. 8 it was a "barren waste." Soldiers had to sleep under blankets in the open air since no tents had arrived nearly two weeks after a decision was made to establish the camp. Confusion was rampant due to a lack of preparations. The ailing soldiers suffered greatly from a lack of proper accommodations and food— their tents had no floors. Only blankets separated the sick men from the ground and "a glass of sour milk apiece was the only nourishment the sick received in 24 hours," noted the *Times*. A doctor who visited the camp found 1,400 troops relied mostly on a stagnant pond for their drinking water. By the end of August, over 20,000 men lived in the camp and 1,300 were in the hospital tents. On Sept. 5, a doctor traveled to the camp with a special train to carry sick soldiers to Brooklyn hospitals but could only transport 15 men due to sightseers using a dozen ambulances on a tour. Ellen's name was on a witness list to attest to mismanagement and abuses at Montauk Point. No doubt these terrible circumstances contributed to Ruby's death—a fact that was obvious in Ellen's writings about the terrible conditions at Camp Wikoff following her daughter's death.

Portrait of Ellen. The Saratoga Springs History Museum.

When Camp Wikoff was vacated at the end of October 1898 some 257 men had died there Ellen's sacrifices at Camp Wikoff and in other facilities during were noticed. She was hailed in leading national newspapers for her tireless work and self-sacrifice credited with saving the lives of soldiers. On Sept. 28, 1899, Ellen was nominated as an honorary member and unanimously elected by the Association of Military Surgeons of the United States in its 8th annual meeting in Kansas City, Mo.

"Her sweet presence and exquisite smile, kind, handsome eyes, and trim, slender figure always will be remembered by the soldiers who were quartered in the hospitals near New York, but it is to be feared that the public will never have an opportunity to become acquainted with the features of this popular heroine of the war, as she has never allowed her photograph to be given to any publication and no authentic photograph of her has ever appeared in print," remarked Etta Ramsdell Goodwin, in an 1898 article *"Woman's Work in the War,"* in *The Chautauquan* magazine.

Although Ruby wasn't entitled to any military survivor benefits as a civilian, the Committee on

Pensions agreed to make an exception at the request of Ellen's friends. A report noted the following.

• Ellen organized the founding of the Woman's National War Relief Association and obtained for it the approbation and backing by the Secretaries of the War and Navy.

• No money raised by her association was used for personal services for herself or Ruby; both served without any compensation.

• Ellen first traveled to field hospitals at Camp Alger (near Falls Church, Va.) to assess their needs.

• She met the first transport of wounded troops arriving at Fort Monroe from Cuba; her supplies were the only ones there for the first week after the men arrived. She spent a month there organizing medical relief, the hospital and nursing staff.

• She traveled to Camp Wikoff to meet the first troops arriving and provided the first hospital supplies. She lived in a tent until the hospital closed. She distributed hospital supplies and food, while coordinating medical relief for the sick and injured.

The report noted that late in life Ellen had been "cut off from the support of a loved and helpful daughter, killed not by the clash of arms, but in a battle requiring more courage and bravery to meet than in the open battlefield." Her friends declared that she deserved a pension as a debt to services rendered—not charity—by herself and her family to be equal to the amount of rank of her father Col. Hardin, who died in battle.

"The irreparable loss of this only companion [Ruby] was not only a great bereavement to the mother, but it deprived her also of her principal means of support," the report stated. The 55th Congress approved granting Ellen a pension in 1899 of $25 per month.

Ellen was described as being in "broken health" after Ruby's demise. In her diary on the date of Ruby's death, Ellen had kept a long lock of Ruby's blonde hair between the pages next to the words "Ruby at her last." Life slowed down then for Ellen, who withstood even more grief after losing yet another child. She occupied her time with activities for DAR and was elected in February 1899 as one of the vice presidents (along with *Ben-Hur* author Lew Wallace) of the Society of American Authors.

In 1912, as honorary vice president general, she attended the DAR's Continental Congress, which drafted resolutions of sympathy, distress and grief at the sinking of the Titanic. The *Evening Star* noted that Ellen, "although very feeble, was in Congress yesterday. She was gowned in black velvet and came down the aisle sharing the applause with the president general, upon whose arm she was leaning very heavily." She also sent in her dollar contribution a month later to help build a women's Titanic memorial.

It is doubtful that her later years were peaceful. She lived part-time in Saratoga and lived with Nelly in Albany and her son Tracy in a Glencarlyn bungalow near Arlington, Va. Census records showed her moving between the various residences. In 1900, Ellen lived with Tracy and again in 1910—she was 77 years old and he was 48. (His occupation was listed as "none.") It must have been difficult for her to watch over her grown son who couldn't hold a steady job, particularly in those times when less was understood about mental illness. Tracy had tried to study medicine at Georgetown and Union colleges, even attending a branch of the School of Physicians and Surgeons at Columbia University. However, he abandoned his studies due to "a feeble constitution." It is likely that he lived off part of an inheritance his uncle Father Clarence left to Ellen's children.

When Tracy later died in December 1928, a headline in the *Evening Star* blared: *"Hermit is Suicide in Virginia Hut—M. Tracy Walworth, Twice Cut in Throat, Once Prominently Connected in D.C."* The newspaper reported he had received medical treatment for cutting his throat with a hunting knife, but had been found dead after he made a second attempt. "According to neighbors, Walworth became mentally unbalanced about three years ago. While riding a bicycle, he crashed into the Post Office building at Glencarlyn and his injuries kept him in a hospital several weeks. A tragedy in his home in early life, it is said, caused him to seek a life of seclusion."

In April 1915, the *Evening Star* reported that Ellen was forced to stay away from that year's Continental Congress due to a "severe attack of the grip" and was confined to her "winter bungalow" with Tracy in

Glencarlyn. This was the first Continental Congress she failed to attend. DAR sent her a bouquet of flowers with a message she was missed.

On June 23, 1915, Ellen passed away at age 83 shortly after midnight at Georgetown University Hospital, where she had been receiving treatment for three weeks. News of her death came as a great shock, particularly for DAR members in Washington, D.C. She buried at Greenridge Cemetery in Saratoga with the Walworth family. In her will ,she wanted her funeral to be conducted by Rev. Carey of the Bethesda Episcopal Church, who presided over her son Frank's funeral. None of her children married, except for Frank. She only left behind one grandchild.

A memorial service was held in her honor at the 1916 Continental Congress. Among the tributes to Ellen was this: "I wish you might have known Mrs. Walworth. The portrait we have upstairs is a very wonderful and an admirable likeness and in it we catch something of the artist's inspiration; but nothing can depict or take the place of the personality, so winning and so wonderful. She lives on beyond the term of life; her children carry on her efforts and her accomplishments; she leaves us a heritage that will go from generation to generation—the heritage of faithful work, of absolute devotion to duty as she saw it, of unfailing readiness to sacrifice when needs arise, and constant fidelity to the highest ideals of our Society, that must bear fruit in the inspiration that she is to every one of us."

In 1940, DAR member Janet E.H. Richards recalled knowing Ellen in the early days of DAR and also from attending one of her parliamentary meetings. She remembered Ellen as an old school intellectual "remarkable for an air of dignified authority and broad culture." Below is a beautiful poem Ellen wrote while visiting her brother Gen. Martin Hardin's home in Florida. It was in the *New York Home Journal* in 1892.

## CASA DEL CAÑONAZA

*Without my window's fair expanse,*
*Spread southern skies of deepest blue,*
*And drifting clouds the scene enhance,*
*Above the bay of azure hue.*
*Close by the window's ledge are seen,*
*A hundred golden balls that bend*
*Beneath their leaves of glistening green,*
*And orange blooms their odors lend.*
*'Twixt tree and bay the barracks stand*
*Where monks their quiet cloister reared;*
*Now soldiers' tread and martial band*
*Sound where the vesper song was heard.*
*The wand of modern life has cast*
*It's spell o'er convent hall and court,*
*As high the flagstaff like a mast,*
*Flings from its shaft the flag in sport.*
*And stern the evening gun reports*
*The day expired, for good or ill,*
*While echoes vibrate from old forts,*
*That of past ages whisper still.*

Portrait of Mary Smith Lockwood by
Aline E. Solomons, DAR librarian general
(painted in 1906 and given to the Mary
Washington Chapter in D.C., which presented
it to the national society). Image courtesy of
DAR.

# Chapter 4: Mary Smith Lockwood

It may be difficult to imagine that one day future generations of women would remember the name of a little girl born in 1831 in a New York wilderness into a family whose children had struggled to survive the premature deaths of their parents for two generations. Her humble origins and early hardships growing up near the shores of Lake Erie, some 60 miles south of Niagara Falls, failed to hold back the keen intellect and literary talent of Mary Smith Lockwood—who someday would be forever known as the pen founder of DAR.

Although a gifted communicator and writer, Mary never really discussed her early life and marriage. Maybe it was too painful and unhappy. Most accounts of her life note her birthday, patriot ancestors and her life after she became a widow. A wide gap of information about her background had existed—until now. The results of careful research below shed light on fascinating aspects of her life that helped define her strong character and future impressive accomplishments.

Unlike the other DAR founders, Mary had no long line of distinguished ancestors, statesmen, lawyers, politicians, or military leaders. She descended from early English colonialists who became ordinary working-class Americans—holding some minor civil posts but mostly supporting themselves through farming, running stores, operating mills, etc., while moving from time to time to seek better circumstances in new frontier settlements.

Her forefather Lt. Samuel Smith sailed from Ipswich, England with his wife and four children in 1634 to help found Wethersfield, Conn.—known as "Ye Most Ancient Towne" in that state. He became a merchant and moved the family to Hadley, Mass. His son Philip Smith (1633–85) gained local prominence. (He is one of Mary's lineal descendants.) Like his father, Philip served as a deputy in the Massachusetts Colony. He became a lieutenant, was appointed to the Town Troop of Hampshire County and served as a deacon as well as a judge in the county court. Today he is also remembered as the 7th example in matters *"Relating the Wonders of the Invisible World in Preternatural Occurrences."* This was in a 1702 a book by Puritan minister/author Cotton Mather called *"Magnalia Christi Americana."*

"He [Philip] was, by his Office, concern'd about relieving the Indigences of a wretched Woman in the Town; who being dissatisfy'd at some of his just Cares about her, express'd her self unto him in such a manner, that he declar'd himself thenceforward apprehensive of receiving Mischief at her hands." He became gravely ill and said he remembered the woman had threatened him.

Cotton Mather by Peter Pelma (1700). Public domain.

As his condition grew worse and he died, suspicions fell on woman due to strange occurrences in the house, including the alleged smell of musk from a rotten apple and illusions of fire on the sick man's bed. Eventually Philip died. The cause was deemed murder by "hideous Witchcraft, that fill'd all those Parts of New England with Astonishment." After his passing, the family continued to live in Hadley for generations. And the accused witch, Mary Webster, was tried and found not guilty.

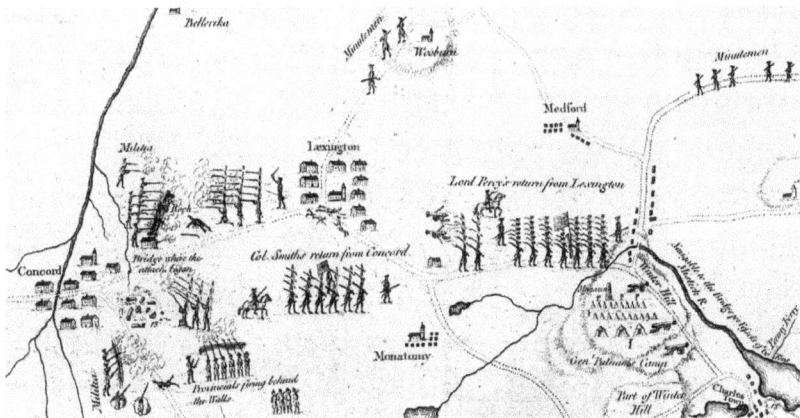

Close up section of a mostly accurate hand-colored map depicting the 1775 Battles of Lexington and Concord, and the Siege of Boston (July 29, 1799). Library of Congress.

Many of Mary's relatives volunteered for short periods of service in militias during the Revolutionary War. The service records of her Massachusetts patriots, the place where most of them came from, are listed in the *Massachusetts Soldiers and Sailors of the Revolutionary War: A Compilation from the*

*Archives,"* published in 1891. It is noteworthy that Massachusetts, compared to other states, provided the most regiments to the Continental Army.

In April 1775, her great-grandfather 47-year-old Benjamin Smith (1728–93) dropped everything to answer a call for arms—the Lexington Alarm—to fight the British days after the Battles of Lexington and Concord on April 19. It was the first military engagement in the Revolutionary War. He became a private under Capt. Perez Graves' Co. Benjamin returned to town after two days' service. The Lexington Alarm occurred before the Continental Congress adopted existing militia forces as its Continental Army in June 1775.

Another one of her great-grandfathers was Ephraim Blodgett (circa 1764–1823) of Brimfield, Mass. He enlisted three times. The first was in March 1779 when he served as a 15-year-old private for three months as a guard in Springfield, Mass., under Capt. John Carpenter's Co. In July 1780, he was among a group raised under Capt. Joseph Browning's Co. He enlisted for three months to reinforce the Continental Army under Col. Seth Murray's Co. (in Hampshire). He was 18 when he enlisted June 16, 1782 as a private in Capt. John Sherman's Co. under Col. Gideon Burt. He marched 20 miles from home in defense of the fledgling American government to fight rioters in Ely's Rebellion at Springfield and Northampton, Mass. In April, nonconformist minister Samuel Ely was hauled to court for sedition and disorderly conduct.

Educated at Yale and born in Connecticut, Ely led protests against the 1780 Massachusetts state constitution in Springfield. He also incited a mob to stop courts from conveying at the Northampton Court of Common Pleas. Armed with a club, Ely incited a mob: "Come on, my brave boys, we'll go to the woodpile and get clubs

Another tax protester, Daniel Shays, a Revolutionary War captain, left, farmers to rebel against taxes in Massachusetts (1787). National Portrait Gallery.

enough and knock their gray wigs off and send them out of the world in an instant." Confessing his guilt, Ely was fined and sentenced to six months imprisonment. He had stirred up local farmers suffering from harsh economic conditions caused by higher taxes, lower prices and an inability to pay debts in cattle as the state government adopted a stronger financial policy to help fight the war. Cases involving debtors filled the court. Blodgett, who served for four days, was among troops sent to stop rioting that began the morning of June 13, 1782 when 130 men busted Ely out of jail.

Mary's early great-grandfathers Benjamin Smith and Daniel Morton Sr. had close ties to Whately, Mass., where they were early settlers. There were no schools for children. The nearest corn mill was five miles away.

From 1765–80, many families moved there because they could buy an acre of land for the price of a pair of shoes, and the terrain was ideal for pastures, noted a *"History of the Town of Whately, Mass"* published in 1899. Benjamin was described as a very prominent citizen who kept the Red Tavern before 1750 and was a justice of the peace. His son Isaac was Mary's grandfather.

On Oct. 26, 1792, Isaac Smith, age 20, wed 18-year-old Roxa Morton. Their eldest child Henry was born the next year. By 1795, Isaac had another son named Benjamin. The young family lived in a two-story house he built on land in the Straits, a main road grid based on an old Native American trail from Umpanchala's fort to the Pocumtuck. A year after the arrival of his fifth child Roxa, born in 1801, the family relocated to Gorham, N.Y., a town founded in 1789 around the Finger Lakes area.

Nathaniel Gorham by Charles Willson Peale (1793). National Park Service.

It is likely that Isaac left his hometown, family and friends in part due to the fame of a state hero Nathaniel Gorham—who sought to make a fortune as a land developer after achieving fame in the Revolutionary War. Who better to trust than Gorham? He started his noteworthy achievements during the fight against the

British by serving on the Board of War. He organized coastal defenses, military expeditions against British bases in Nova Scotia, and the Continental Army's logistics when it left Massachusetts for New York. He was a state delegate to the first constitutional convention (1779–80) and served both as a two-term member and president of the Continental Congress. After the war, Gorham and another businessman used their influence and funds to buy from the Commonwealth of Massachusetts 2.6 million acres of wilderness in western New York. The land was sold to settlers like Isaac Smith. But the deal ruined Gorham when he couldn't pay for the real estate after the value of paper money (scrip) rose—inflating the original $1 million paid in devalued Massachusetts. Nevertheless, the town where Smith made a farming homestead was named in Gorham's honor.

Isaac worked the land there for eight years. He grew his family and had a total of nine children:

- Henry Benjamin—born 1793 (Mary's father),
- Benjamin E.—1794,
- Matilda—1796,
- Rodney Barnes—1798/99,
- Roxa—1801,
- Tirzah—1804,
- Hiram—1807,
- Atteley—1809,
- Esther—1811.

Circumstances must have been unfavorable in Gorham because in 1810 Isaac moved the family

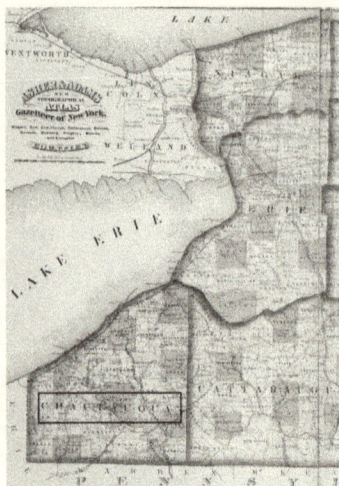

Part of a map showing Chautauqua County (1871). New York Public Library.

125 miles in the opposite direction across western New York to the shoreline town of Sheridan, located in Chautauqua County along the Lake Erie coastline. Poverty is the likely cause for the move. The area was still largely unpopulated. During the Revolutionary War, frontier settlements in western New York had been raided by hostile Native Americans and British troops. Peace came to the area following U.S. government treaties with tribes in 1795. When the isolated Chautauqua County was offered for sale around 1800, acreage there was the least expensive and didn't cost as much as other places in New York that had fertile land for farms. Those frontier settlers of Chautauqua County "were the poorest class of people—men who often expended their last dollar to procure the article for their land," noted *"History of Chautauqua County, New York"* by Andrew White Young (1875).

To settle there you had to be among the heartiest frontier pioneers "accustomed to wield the axe and handle the rifle; who could grapple with the forest, and rough it in the wilderness, and think it ease; who could reap the thin harvest, and live upon the coarse and often scanty fare of the woods, and call it plenty; consequently the first settlers of this county were mostly from the backwoods region, at the western verge of settlement." How different this land must have seemed to the Smith family—so far away from their loved ones in such a harsh, wild environment compared to colonial Massachusetts.

A biography of Rodney Barnes Smith remarked, "The country was then almost an entire wilderness; and the hardships of pioneer life were the lot of the [Smith] family." In the Sheridan area, the Smiths lived in a rented small log cabin a mile from Forestville. Isaac was able to save money to move again nearby and continued to struggle to survive. Earlier settlers also lived in fear of attack by neighboring Iroquois. Indian paths provided transportation routes until the first road was surveyed in the county in 1813 and built.

By August 1811, Isaac moved five miles away to another new wilderness town called Hanover, where he bought a western parcel of land. Living in great isolation without village infrastructure, roads or law enforcement, settlers had to report twice each year for militia training at Buffalo. He started to build a mill there to earn money to supplement farming.

The Smith family would undergo greater hardships as hostilities with the British in nearby Canada unfolded during the War of 1812. Although war had not yet been declared, President James Madison called on several states to raise troops in April 1812. An order was issued

April 21, 1812 for New York to provide 13,500 men to serve immediate in the state militia. According to an act of Congress passed in March 1809, each and every free and able-bodied male between the ages of 18 and 45 "shall

Regular Army uniform in the War of 1812 (1905). New York Public Library.

severally and respectively be enrolled in the militia by the captain or commanding officer of the company within whose bounds such citizen reside." In addition, each militiaman had to arm himself within six months of being enrolled with the following items:

• A good musket or firelock, a sufficient bayonet and belt, two spare flints, a knapsack, a pouch with a box having at least musket/firelock 24 cartridges and the correct amount of powder and ball, or

• A good rifle, knapsack, shot-pouch and powder horn, 20 rifle balls and a quarter of a pound of power, and shall appear so armed; and

• Officers must be equipped with a sword and spontoon (polearm).

The war began June 18, 1812. "Volunteers were called for, the militia was drafted, the forts upon the seaboard were garrisoned, privateers were fitted out and sent to sea, troops were hurried forward to the norther border; and the President, Congress and governors of states actively cooperated in offensive and defensive preparations," noted the *"History of the Seventh Regiment of New York, 1806-1889"* by Emmons Clark (1890). U.S. authorities began a dialogue with the Senecas in Buffalo, who agreed to side with the Americans, while the Mohawks backed the British. During the War of 1812, New York supplied 77,896 men.

At the start of the war, New York was to provide 50,000 militia volunteers as a state quota. Chautauqua County, whose residents numbered 3,000, raised a militia in July 1812 that merged with Col. Hugh W. Dobbin's Regiment. Historical writings and documents reveal that many of these frontiersmen had no military training. They were poorly fed, received much lower wages than laborers, suffered from a lack of basic provisions in harsh snowy winters and often walked away to return home when they thought they'd fulfilled their brief enlistment terms—without proper military authorization. These factors and others led to high numbers of desertions. But having a record for deserting apparently didn't bother many of the frontiersmen there, who were "tenacious of their rights as citizens, and often insubordinate," according to *"History of Chautauqua County, New York, and Its People,"* Vol. 1, Eds. John P. Downs and Fenwick Y. Hedley (1921). It noted that they would leave if their term was over no matter if it happened during a critical time in the military campaign. Militia volunteers enlisted for six months or a year and received from

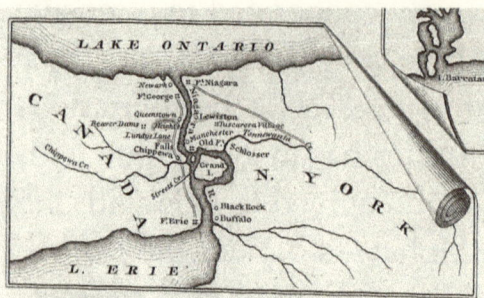

Close up of Niagara frontier, one of five principal seats in the War of 1812 from *"Willard's History of the United States,"* (1828). Library of Congress.

$5 to $10 per month form the U.S. government. Some earned extra (a bounty) for clothes and weapons.

The Niagara frontier area where the family lived was caught in the constant military tug-of-war between both sides. The *Buffalo Gazette* (N.Y.) provided important insights Dec. 15, 1812 on conditions there which impacted the Smith family, who lived less than 45 miles south of Buffalo. It noted that citizens lived in constant fear from enemies, famine and contagious epidemics. British soldiers and their Indian allies were notorious for burning, plundering and destroying American property in raids crossing over from Canada onto U.S. soil along the Niagara frontier. Problems transporting goods into the area meant a shortage of goods and high prices. "The taverns and groceries are completely dried up. Even the whiskey distilleries are very hard run," stated the *Gazette,* adding that new militia volunteers suffered from "violent colds" while living in tents in the winter.

American Brig. Gen. George McClure on Dec. 10, 1813 ordered the village of Newark in Canada burned after American troops abandoned nearby Fort George following its capture from the

British. This aggressive act against innocent civilians caused much condemnation by Americans and British alike. England's officers were outraged at the crime. Everyone knew retaliation would come.

Brig. Gen. McClure, commander of the Niagara frontier, hastened back over the Canadian border to his headquarters in Buffalo. Three days after burning Newark, he became alarmed by what the British would do. He issued a warning to the residents of Chautauqua and two other counties. "The present crisis is alarming," he declared, warning families to flee to safer areas and men to take up arms to defend the land, homes and country from an impending attack. The British rampaged against Fort Niagara.

Isaac was among other volunteers. The exact details of his enlistment and service are unknown. His name doesn't appear on the lists with other militia recruits from Chautauqua County, nor are there pension records or land bounties tied specifically to him. However biographies about his relatives mention his service as a private in the War of 1812 and claim he was among those trying to defend Buffalo from the British in December 1813. Isaac, age 41, could have been among a few companies of Niagara Frontier volunteers composed of older male recruits called the "Silver Greys." One possibility is that he was the Private Isaac Smith who served with Col. Philetus Swift's Detachment (1812–13) there at the same time in Buffalo. It is unknown if Isaac already served in a militia or was among the 400

men in four companies from
Chautauqua who packed arms
and marched in December to
fight the British and their Native
American allies around Buffalo.
This unit was the 162 Regiment
led by Col. John McMahan. On
Dec. 26, 1813, Isaac would
have been among 2,000
volunteer troops "of all
descriptions" stationed at
Buffalo and the immediate
vicinity, its commander
Maj. Gen. Amos Hall described to
N.Y. Gov. Daniel D. Tompkins.

Amos Hall in
Members of the
N.Y. House of Assembly
(1798). National
Portrait Gallery.

It didn't take long for the British to react. Early
on the morning of Dec. 30, over 1,500 troops crossed
the Niagara River, landing their boats half a mile
south of Fort Gibson at Black Rock, which derived
its name from black limestone that used to be along
the waterfront by Buffalo. Their goal was to capture
American supplies and equipment at a depot in Black
Rock, N.Y., the site of a ferry and a small boat wharf.
The Chautauqua volunteers were inside log huts a
short distance from Buffalo opposite the shoreline as
British soldiers and 400 Natives crept over. An alarm
was raised at midnight about the enemy's approach,
but the Americans didn't know the enemy troops
already landed—resulting in confusion, surprise
and organizational disarray. Maj. Gen. Hall ordered

an attack. However, the British had already crossed the Niagara River and taken a bridge. An American cavalry detachment tried to prevent a further advance until gun bursts from the British caused the cavalry to panic and flee—riding over their own infantry in the rear. American troops scattered.

In addition to the soldiers around Buffalo, the citizens were also taken by surprise. In 1870, Martha St. John Skinner remembered her experiences as a little girl on the night the town burned. Her tale is preserved in the Buffalo History Museum.

Martha St. John Skinner as an adult from "Buffalo Historical Society Publications," Vol. 9 (1905).

*"... a great number of troops... marched to Black Rock [and] all the people felt safe ... [we] were sitting up at our house listening to hear the guns at Black Rock supposing we were safe, when suddenly the alarm gun boomed up with such an awful burst of thunder as aroused everybody and people were flying every way for safety; we were soon prepared for a start & Mr. Bemis whose house was opposite ours ... (he being able with his wagon horses to carry his family and part of ours) so we were all packed in three girls and three boys with beds blankets and clothing, and he drove out Main street until he came to North street. There we met our Seneca Indians retreating and the Canadian Indians pursuing and firing on them. The bullets*

came whistling by us, and Mr. Bemis not liking the music, turned ... and drove back... [He] said to my Mother that he would be compelled to go the other road on the lake shore, but he would return as soon as possible and take away the remainder of the family.

"But as we passed the head of Niagara street, which was the place of the alarm gun, we looked down the road and saw the British army arrayed on Niagara Square, and a person before them on horseback facing them holding a white flag over his shoulder ... . When we arrived at the ferry one mile up the creek called Pratts ferry, we were compelled to wait our turn to cross, the ice was not thick enough to drive over although people could walk across.

"After crossing, we drove up the Lake shore, the people came flying by us some [went one] way some another. There was Mrs Atkins, who had fallen off the horse in to the

Refugees on the Niagara frontier in the War of 1812 by Stanley Arthurs (1905). New York Public Library.

quicksand with her baby. We came to Mr. Barker's tavern 8 miles from Buffalo. Mrs. Barker was very sick and died the 10th of Jan. We pursued our Journey ... as we were waiting for our way over the creek, we saw the smoke of the burning village coming over the trees so we knew it would be of no use to return..."

Maj. Gen. Hall ordered a retreat to try to use his remaining troops to protect Buffalo, but to no avail. The British burned homes and buildings and marched two miles onto Buffalo where they torched everything except the jail and house of a resident Margaret St. John. American forces were able to attack later as the British attempted to cross the river back to Canada with their plunder.

"At daylight the Chautauqua regiment [held as a reserve in battle] was ordered to advance, they proceeded down the river nearly half a mile...where, after a sharp contest with the enemy in force, they broke as the body of militia had done before. Some fled disgracefully, while others behaved well and tried to rally the men. ... Through the woods a portion of the Chautauqua regiment as well as portions of the other American forces fled followed by the Indians who filled the woods and killed and scalped many of the flying troops," noted a Chautauqua County Historical Society document on the battle.

Isaac was among those who left Buffalo after the attack and returned to their nearby homes—either in the retreat or among the many deserters. One account in the *"History of Chautauqua County, New York"* claims he served in the Navy, was involved in "the disaster of Buffalo" and caught a fatal fever during a forced march from Buffalo. Another book *"History of Chautauqua County, New York: From its First Settlement to the Present Time"* also repeats he was forced to march from Buffalo to his home after the town's burning. What all accounts agree on is that he became sick at some point during his return and died afterwards. It is said Isaac caught a fever and died at home in 1814. Soldiers who became ill often went home on furlough. It appears his family received

The Burning of Buffalo from *"Pictorial History of America,"* by Samuel G. Goodrich (1847). New York Public Library.

no pension for his service. A meeting of the N.Y. State Legislature in January 1814 noted that many families of state militia soldiers who died at Black Rock (another name for the Burning of Buffalo) were wounded or disabled as a result were unlikely to qualify then for any government financial support. This must have been a huge blow to his family. His 40-year-old widow Roxa Morton Smith then became the head of the family of nine children. The eldest was 23-year-old Henry (Mary's Smith Lockwood's father) and the youngest Esther, age four.

Within one year of Isaac's passing, Roxa died some time before the war ended on Feb. 18, 1815. Henry was now the head of the family of orphans. Wanting his baby sister to be properly cared for, Henry carried little Esther (a toddler) in his arms as he trekked over 100 miles with the child's clothing and food to his aunt Mrs. William Mather in Gorham, N.Y. It was an incredible journey especially because Henry traversed most of the way without any roads. Not long afterward, the Mathers were unable to care for Esther and gave her to a couple from New York City.

One of the first log cabins in the county, from "History of Chautauqua County, and its People," (1921).

The Smiths lived through years of great hardship and poverty that extended during the war and for several years after their parents died. The summer of 1816, for instance, was long remembered for frigid temperatures that caused ice to form every month that year. "July was accompanied by frost and ice; the 'Fourth' was cold and raw; blustering winds swept the entire Atlantic coast. On the 5th, ice was formed as thick as window glass in New York City and Pennsylvania. In August, ice half an inch thick was frequently seen. Flowers froze, corn was killed, and all attempts to raise other crops were abandoned," the *History of Chautauqua County*" noted. In that year, Henry's first child was born. He and Benjamin both married daughters of Ephraim Blodgett of Massachusetts, who served in the Revolutionary War. Henry first married Beulah Blodgett, age 16, in Buffalo on Oct. 19, 1815.

Benjamin wed her younger sister Achsah in 1819.

The family then endured the "Starving Season," as the first half of 1817 came to be known. High prices—flour at $18 per barrel, potatoes for $1.50 a bushel—coupled with low wages for laborers (60 cents per day) meant that most people in Western New York lived for a year on greens they could find or hunted wild game. Economic times improved following the building of the Erie Canal (1817–25) as an important commercial and passenger route linking Buffalo with Albany.

Henry worked hard. He built a sawmill and flour mills, a large tannery and a store. His brothers shared in the business activities. They were able to create Smith's Mills, and he maintained a close relationship with his brothers. Henry enjoyed enough financial prosperity to live in a framed house rather than a log cabin. He and Beulah welcomed seven children into their family:

- Julia Ann (1816–1829),
- Sally Adelia (1818–1854),
- Emaline (1820–1871),
- Henry M. Smith (1822–1827),
- Susan Catherine Smith (1825–1877),
- Rodney Brown Smith (1827–1902),
- Mary Smith (1831–1922).

After the family was financially secure in 1823, Henry's brother Rodney was sent to find Esther and bring her home. She rejoined her siblings at age 12. Smith's Mills became a post-hamlet in Hanover township on the Erie Railroad and was located about 12 miles east of Dunkirk. When Ephraim Blodgett died in 1823, his widow moved in with Henry, Beulah and their children. The completion of the Erie Canal ended the pioneer phase. The area became more prosperous as the county's population increased to 44,800 inhabitants by 1835. People no longer had to live in log cabins. They could build houses with boards cut at Smith's Mills. The year Mary was born marked a boon in lumbering—which raised the standard of living for the Smith brothers and their families.

Henry became involved in local politics. In 1836, he was among five delegates from the town of Hanover at the Whig County Convention for Chautauqua County. Mary later said she learned and became interested in politics from her father. Smith's Mills continued to grow. It became an important livestock freight station for the New York & Erie Railroad Co. Boards and shingles were shipped to be sold in Pittsburgh, Cincinnati, Louisville and as far away as New Orleans. The county even had enough money to create a poorhouse run by community leaders to help the needy. Public buildings and a jail were built.

Mary's uncle, Rodney Brown Smith "History of Chautauqua County, New York," (1875).

279

Map of Hanover, N.Y. (1867).

Schools and the education of children became emphasized. People had more money to dress better and participate in leisurely activities. In this comfortable community environment, Mary was raised and went to school. Her uncles had done well.

Uncle Rodney became a subcontractor on Big Rock dam and a contractor for the Erie Canal. He even built a plank road in 1852 connecting the mills to Jamestown and several towns, including Hanover. He operated a distillery and tannery at Smith's Mills. Uncle Hiram focused on agriculture and farming. In 1854, Smith's Mills even had its own post office. Her family lived a quiet life. The only notoriety occurred when Mary was four. *"Extraordinary Youthful Depravity"*—blared the *Buffalo Patriot and Commercial Advertiser.* It recounted an assault committed by Uncle Hiram's five-year-old son, who stabbed four-year-old son of Abner Blodgett, in the side with a pocketknife in a quarrel Jan. 20, 1836 during a snowball fight. Blodgett failed to heed the warning that "if he threw another snowball he [Smith] would cut his head off or kill him." The fate of the injured child is unknown but news reports said the "wound was so severe that the boy became immediately speechless." Little hope was expected for recovery.

By the time Mary was born, Henry and Beulah had suffered the loss of their eldest Julia Ann (who died at 13) and middle child Henry M., five. The only surviving son was Rodney Brown Smith (named after his uncle); he was four years older than Mary. She maintained a special relationship with him. Only four years old when Beulah died in 1838, Mary wrote of her devotion to Rodney in a book dedication in 1889.

### To My Brother, Rodney B. Smith:

*"When you read this page of dedication and see to whom it is inscribed, your first thought will be of the days so long ago, when hand in hand, we climbed the hills and spanned the meadow brooks, because we were 'nest-deserted birds grown chill through something wanting' in our home. Of all that such a recollection implies, the saddest and sweetest to both of us, we could not speak, one to the other, without voices faltering. It is enough that each doth know the other's thought.*

*"The boyish arm that round me clung in those sad days, has stronger grown as years have passed, in manly might, softening or enhancing the bitter or the good that each has known. To you I give this inscription, knowing my heart will be satisfied; for between me and the public I shall have, at least, one generous reader."*

—Mary Smith Lockwood,

*"Historic Homes in Washington: Its Noted Men and Women"*

Henry remarried quickly. The U.S. Census for 1840 reveals that two years after Beulah died, he was living in a household with Mary, Rodney and apparently their stepmother Candace, who was two years older than her husband. There is only one woman in her 40s living in the household (Candace would have been 48 or 49), and no mention of his widowed mother-in-law (58 years old) although she had been living among the family. (Sybil Blodgett likely moved in with another relative since she died in 1854 at age 72 in the same town.) Not only did the children lose a mother in the household, but their grandmother, too.

Given Mary's book dedication, it is obvious there was no close relationship with Candace, a native of Vermont, who had already lived within the small community for a decade. Such a moving and melancholy remembrance of her childhood with Rodney indicates their home was far from loving after their mother died. When the next census was taken in 1850, Mary would have been 19 years old. Records indicate she and Rodney had moved out by then. Some accounts say Mary taught school nearby in a village called Brocton when she became an adult. A later biography stated that Mary's education in Hanover was typical of that time—slate and quill pens. She apparently loved to read, which no doubt provided a firm foundation for her later success as an esteemed author.

Wedding bells rung for her on Sept. 15, 1851 when she married Henry C. Lockwood (who shared the same the first name as her father). His father Charles Lockwood, a druggist who ran a combination apothecary and grocery store, was an important man in towns of Hanover and Silver Creek. It's nearly impossible to read an issue of the Jamestown Journal (a local leading newspaper) after 1849 without seeing his name in advertisements as an agent of medicinal tonics. For *Jamestown Journal*, Feb. 9, 1849. instance, he was an agent in 1849 for "*Dr. Guysott's Compound Extract of Yellow Dock and Sarsaparilla*" prepared at S.F. Bennett's Laboratory in N.Y. Selling per quart at $1 a bottle or six for $5, it was a popular remedy made of sarsaparilla, yellow dock [herb] and vegetables "united in such proportions that they cause a simultaneous, harmonious and energetic effort of the whole system to throw off disease, so that while one organ is stimulated to throw off its impurities and obstructions, all the other organs are proportionably active, and these impurities and obstructions instead of finding a new resting placed, are carried completely out of the system." It was touted to cure liver complaints, dyspepsia, nervous affections, corrupt humors, colds, asthma, body pains and mercurial diseases. It was advertised as "the best female medicine known." Charles Lockwood also became authorized to sell "*Dr. G.C. Vaughn's*

---

*Vegetable Lithontriptic Mixture"*—a celebrated remedy for family use to treat dropsy, diseases of the organs and debility of the system. His business must have been good because the 1850 Census showed him to be a wealthy merchant (compared to others) with real estate valued at $2,000. Another indication of his high standing in the community was an August 1853 appointment to the Grand Jury in the Chautauqua County Circuit Court and Court of Oyer and Terminer.

The Smith and Lockwood children grew up together. Charles Lockwood (whose father David from Connecticut served with Col. John Lamb's regiment in the Revolutionary War) brought his family over from Rochester to Hanover. The Census in 1840 shows Charles and his wife Elisabeth (both born in 1805 in Connecticut) had five children. Mary and her beloved brother Rodney each married a Lockwood. She was the first. He followed sometime afterwards and wed Ann Maria Lockwood who was the same age as he.

Little is known about Mary's early wedded life. In 1855, she still lived in the community. Henry, two years older, was listed as a clerk in the Census records. Mary was then 23 years old. At that time, she had taken her 11-year-old niece Sophia DeWolf into their home. The child's mother Sally Adelia Smith DeWolf (who had five young children) had died the year before. [Mary's final resting place would be shared in the same grave with Sophia's married daughter Jessie Christiancy and her husband.]

Five years later, Mary and Henry remained in the area. By then they had become parents to son Rodney C. Lockwood, born in 1856.

Henry's career path is a strange one. He is listed in a New York state business directory from 1859 as working for sawmill operator E.R. Ballard & Co. He seems to have gone from one type of job to another.

In 1861, Mary and Henry followed Rodney to Elmira, N.Y. Her brother had attended Fredonia Academy and started his career as a merchant in Silver Spring before moving to Elmira in 1854. A city director notes that Rodney was the manufacturer of a grain cleaner and lived in a house on 50 William—the same address as Henry. After the Civil War began, Rodney moved with his wife to Baltimore in 1862. Rather than join the military, Rodney backed the Union and remained as a businessman based there with dealings in Norfolk, Va., and New Bern, N.C.

Mention has been made that Mary and Henry lived in Washington, D.C. during the Civil War. One account claims he was an officer in the Union Army. However, there was another officer of the same name whose identity could have been mistaken for Mary's husband. Instead it is more likely that Henry was a sutler who sold merchandise, food and other provisions to the Army. Given the closeness between Mary and her brother Rodney, he continued to lend a hand to her husband in the business world. While Mary and Henry may have traveled from Baltimore to D.C. during the Civil War, Henry was called a sutler in *"Woods' Baltimore City Directory"* (1864–66).

Mary and her husband made their home in Baltimore. In May 1867, a classified ad in *The Baltimore Sun* revealed that Henry and Rodney had been part of a partnership called Smith, Dixon & Lockwood, an early manufacturer of paper bags in the United States and twine.

Henry did not have the same gift for business that Rodney did. Although his occupation is listed as commerce and a merchant in the 1870 Census, he did not possess the wealth of other clerks and merchants mentioned on the same page. Instead, the value of his personal estate is listed at $1,200 (the same as a clerk) and there is a blank space for the value of his real estate. A business directory describes him as a paper-bag manufacturer.

This financial situation must have been hard for Mary, who appears as the new mother of baby Lillian. Her first child Rodney must have died by then because he is not in any records after the 1856 Census.

Henry had a creative streak, perhaps like his father who mixed experimental concoctions as druggists did in those days. He decided to become an inventor. He struck out on his own and formed a "Coffee Renovater" company called L & Co. located on 61 Thames in Baltimore in 1872. It was described as a coffee cleaning mill in a partnership with wholesale grocer H. Tinsley.

He was granted U.S. patents for:

• A paper bag machine on March 9, 1869, No. 87,689,

- A coffee cleaner and polisher on Jan. 25, 1870, No. 99,215,
- A railway car wheel on Nov. 14. 1871, No. 120,985,
- Adjustable and detachable straps for garments (an elastic waist strap for pantaloons, with a triangular buckle and attaching button-holed tabs) on Dec. 19, 1871, No. 122,038,
- "The Tin-Foil" patent to improve coffee packages on Aug. 23, 1873, No. 142,248,
- A coffee roaster on Dec. 23, 1873, No. 145,880,
- A dredge can to contain spices and other pulverized substances on March 25, 1874, No. 148,472.

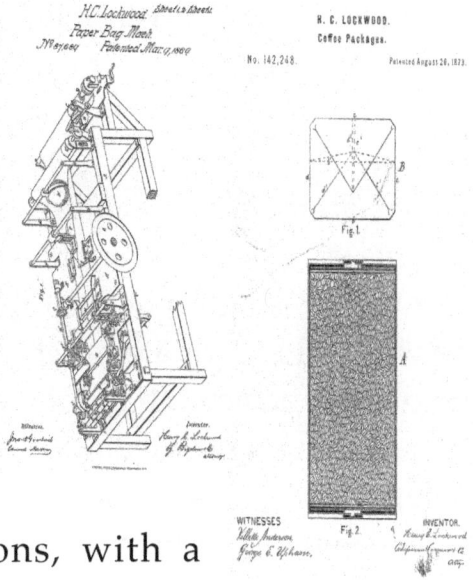

HENRY C. LOCKWOOD.

Adjustable and Detachable Straps for Garments.

No. 122,038.    Patented Dec. 19, 1871.

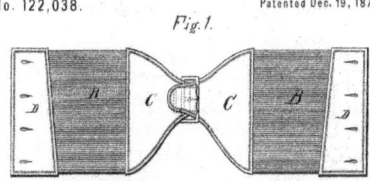

148,472.—Dredge - Can.—HENRY C. LOCKWOOD, Baltimore, Md. Application filed November 29, 1873.

The lid of the can has a small opening; to the center of the lid a plate is pivoted, which has perforations so as to register with the opening; projections on the lid and concavities in the plate held the parts in connection.

Claim.—The holding projection e' on perforated cover B, in combination with concavities e in the circularly-adjustable and perforated plate or cap C of a dredge-can, constructed substantially as described.

In 1874, he turned his attention to doing business in spices and appears listed among eight others competitors in the same field. His address was 11 Commerce, and he was still involved in the coffee business. Henry's home life must have been chaotic

287

with his flurry of inventing activity—from creating an article of clothing, a wheel, a paper bag machine, a spice container and devices for coffee production. To prepare the documents to submit to the U.S. Patent Office, an inventor would have to pay fees for the patents, attorneys and engravings. Within five years, Henry had sought patents on seven items. Perhaps he was looking for a get-rich-quick invention. If so, he did not achieve that goal. When his 74-year-old father Charles Lockwood died on Nov. 26, 1876 in Baltimore, Henry—the eldest son—did not handle any arrangements nor host the funeral. Instead, Mary's brother, the dependable Rodney, took charge. Rodney held the funeral in his living room in his residence at on 431 Madison Ave. Not only that, but Rodney also took and supported Lucy Jane Lockwood (the eldest, an unmarried daughter/sister to his wife and brother-in-law Henry) until her death in 1890.

In 1875–76, Henry's occupation reverted to being a clerk by the time he was in his mid-40s. A year later he traveled to Lincoln, Neb., possibly in the company of Mary and their youngster Lillian, to be among the six family pallbearers for the funeral of Susan Catherine Smith Keith, who died in September 1877 at age 52. The service for Mary's elder sister was held at the Railroad Hotel where Episcopal preacher F.E. Bullard and a choir sang her favorite hymns, "Nearer My God to Thee" and "Rock of Ages." Mrs. Keith and her husband were early Nebraska pioneers, with Keith County named in his honor.

After that time, Henry is never mentioned again. One wonders what Mary thought of her husband's erratic business dealings. Their lack of children could have been a sign of marital discord. But a better indication is what happened when Henry died and afterwards. It is almost as if he never existed. He doesn't appear to be buried in the same Baltimore cemetery where his father, sister, Rodney B. Smith and their other relatives are buried. If he had died in Baltimore, the person likely to handle the arrangements would have been Rodney. Yet, Mary rarely spoke of her husband at all after 1878 when she was a widow who moved from Baltimore to Washington, D.C. In fact, her years in Baltimore don't appear to be mentioned by her at all. This is curious because it was there she launched her career as an author—no doubt aided by her brother.

One of her earlier works, under her initials rather than full name, was dedicated to R.B.S. (brother Rodney). It is a *"Hand-Book of Ceramic Art,"* by M.S. Lockwood (1877) written while her husband was alive and when they were in Baltimore. The impetus for this book, retold later by an acquaintance, came from the fact that Mary sought high and low for a book she could read to learn about the history of ceramics. Being unable to find one, she penned it herself. Her book was well received and mentioned frequently in other publications. It launched her career as a historian and author.

She followed that work with,*"Art Embroidery: A Treatise on the Revived Practice of Decorative*

Decorative needlework samples Mary included in her book, with advice about which to use for quilts, curtains, footstool covers, etc.

*Needlework"*(1878) that she coauthored under her initials with Elizabeth Glaister and artist Thomas Crane. It expounded upon the principles that needlework should:

• Express intelligence and give evidence of the direct application of the mind to the material;

• Be in every way adapted to the materials used;

• Satisfy requirements both of use and beauty.

What is extraordinary about this book are its inclusion of 19 colored samples of lovely artistic embroidery. These provide designs for footstools, cushions, quilts, tablecloths, curtains, tea towels and piano decorations. Reviews were positive. "On the whole, this volume may be of use to some, and of interest to many, whilst the book is so beautifully got up, that it will be a welcome addition to the drawing room table; but we consider that the subject has not been exhaustively treated, and that there is still room for much useful writing upon it," wrote *Industrial Art* magazine in 1877.

By the time Henry passed away, Mary was already on her way to becoming a successful author. The book topics were not controversial, appealing to homemakers. That changed. Freed from her marriage by the death of Henry, she abandoned the prospect of a comfortable (and boring) life living with her brother and extended family. Instead she chose to make it on her own in the nation's capital. She could have taken a less risky option and stayed in Baltimore. Alternatively she could have found another husband to support her and Lillian (Lily). That's not what she wanted. Once a widow, she finally became her own woman at age 47—and seized the moment.

Mary Smith Lockwood—rather than Mrs. Henry Lockwood—was born when she moved to Washington, D.C. in 1878. Like her brother, father and uncles before, Mary was shrewd at business. She decided to work for herself and became manager of The Strathmore Arms boarding house, in central district at Nos. 808, 810 and 812 12th St. N.W. As a single mother, she raised eight-year-old Lily there while creating an intellectual and cultural salon for women, politicians, diplomats, legislators, professors, and writers.

The Strathmore Arms offered both "permanent or transient" board. Those who stayed longer were described as having "taken parlors." In 1884, for example, N.Y. Rep. Aaron Van Schaick Cochrane and former Chicago postmaster Frank Palmer were among those with parlors at the Strathmore Arms. It was four stories high. A center staircase connected to sleeping rooms on the second, third and fourth floors.

President James Garfield (1880). National Portrait Gallery.

Not long after establishing herself in Washington, D.C., Mary found herself caught up in a notorious trial in November 1881 for the murder of President James Garfield, fatally shot to death at a train station July 2, 1881 by a mentally ill man named Charles Julius Guiteau. Mary had met Guiteau about four months before the killing when he wanted to rent a room at the Strathmore Arms. Because none were available, he stayed elsewhere but agreed to eat his meals there. Mary took the witness stand in the trial. She described how Guiteau was unable to pay his bill. They exchanged notes on the matter, with him promising to pay. "It's of no consequence," he interrupted during her testimony, "I was there for a month, and I paid them $5 on account. That's all there is about it. A very nice lady—a very nice lady, indeed," reported the *Evening Star* on Nov. 23, 1881. "They were too kind-hearted and too polite to annoy me about my board. ...a good place to board." When asked about his demeanor, Mary told the court he seemed eccentric, nervous and lacked knowledge of proper etiquette. "There were people at the table that I don't know anything about, and of course I kept my mouth shut. I don't talk to people I know nothing about," he replied. "Gen. [John Alexander] Logan boarded there and a lot of high-toned people. I can recommend it as a boarding house." When questioned further, she said some patrons complained about his behavior; he would turn away suddenly and looking at a person "in a very disagreeable manner." Guiteau's reply to this was because his eyes were "pretty sharp." The defendant was convicted of murder in January 1882 and sentenced to hang. Before the execution, he was allowed to recite a poem he wrote called "I am going to the Lordy." Mary never spoke about the Guiteau incident publicly.

Charles Julius Guiteau (1881). Library of Congress.

Her pet project was the Travel Club, which she organized in January 1881 from her home at the Strathmore Arms. Her idea was to study foreign countries (including music, culture, history, literature, art and geography) from the perspective of recent travelers. People who had been abroad were invited to her soirees to give talks and read papers with entertainment (mostly songs and music) played from the different nations. Participants also enjoyed refreshments she provided. A notice was sent in advance of each meeting. From 1886 to 1889, featured countries included Germany, France, Sweden, Norway and Egypt. Patrons of her Travel Club were

Sara Jane Lippincott (1872). National Portrait Gallery.

often mentioned in D.C. newspapers—Gen. Logan, House Speaker Thomas Reed of Maine, Secretary of State John Watson Foster, and journalist Sara Jane Lippincott (the first woman correspondent for *The New York Times* whose pen name was Grace Greenwood). This love of knowledge, intellectual curiosity and sense of adventure expanded her horizons beyond being the dutiful housewife of the past. It is remarkable that her interests in travel were so great considering she did not visit Europe until 1910. Later in life she traveled across the U.S. and coast-to-coast in 1894 with the Women's National Press Association of which she was president.

It was in this refined boarding house that Mary's activities to advance women's rights awakened. Known as a D.C. pioneer of woman's suffrage, Mary later said in April 1897 that her interest in women's rights happened after she heard a speech given by Phoebe Cousins (both the first woman lawyer and U.S. Marshal) in Lincoln Hall in 1879.

Despite her limited formal education, she amassed important knowledge from her surroundings in the nation's capital and the people she rubbed elbows with. She came to know and work with many women leading suffrage movements. She

Mary Smith Lockwood (1916). Library of Congress.

was described in 1893 as "physically slight, but strong, and rather below the medium height. She has firmness, strength and executive ability of a high order. An interesting face, with character written on the broad bow, and in the deep blue eyes of intellectual sweetness there is mingled a determination of purpose and firm resolve. Her hair, silvered and wavy, shades a face, full of kindly interest in humanity. Her voice has a peculiar charm, low-keyed and musical, yet sympathetic and far-reaching. She is friendly to all progressive movements, especially in the progress of woman," according to *American Monthly*.

Her thoughts about writing allude to prejudice and sexism that women authors faced.

"Correspondence and even editorship has risen to a profession among women, and with the exception of a small minority who do not find the circulation of scandals and misstatements in any sense profitable, they are generously rewarded," Mary declared in her *"Historic Homes"* book. "Women, as a rule, write from a conscientious love of their work, and they become popular in proportion as their style differs from the rough rhetoric of their brother bohemians. Their energy and perseverance is making the profession a permanent avocation for women, and as the press grows in influence, more and more will it require the wit, grace and sparkle that emanate from intellectual womanhood."

—THE—

# Historic Homes

—IN—

## WASHINGTON.

### ITS NOTED MEN and WOMEN.
Fully Illustrated.
BY
**Mary S. Lockwood.**

Orders received at the Publishers' Headquarters in Washington,
**810 12th St., and at Brentannos.**
Address M. S. LOCKWOOD, 810 12th street, Wash
ington, D. C., for full information of terms to Agents.
Mention The Home Magazine.

*Cawker City Public Record* (Kan., May 22, 1890.

Women seeking a place to meet in various organizations and for feminist causes found a welcome place with Mary. The Woman's National Press Association, formed in 1882, was one group that met there and made its headquarters in Washington, D.C.. Not long afterwards Mary S. Lockwood became its president and members included Clara Barton. The Strathmore Arms in 1888 also hosted a theatrical performance to benefit the Women's Education and

Industrial Union. The next year the District Woman's Suffrage Association met; a paper was read about the importance of observing parliamentary order in women's meetings. That same group also met there to plan a school contest to award $5 and $10 prizes to eighth-grade students who could write the best essays on woman suffrage. In 1891, the New England Women's Press Club of Boston frequented the Strathmore Arms.

With a pen in hand, she became a gifted writer who contributed to magazines and wrote books. Her talents and views on women's rights in journalism can be found in her book, *"Historic Homes in Washington"* (1889). Her book received glowing reviews. "This is a fertile field, and it is surprising that no one has entered it before and undertaken what Mrs. Lockwood has accomplished so thoroughly and so well. Her work includes the most prominent social and political events of the century, sketches

U.S. Treasury (1891). Library of Congress.

of the people who have taken part in them, and the houses which have events of peculiar interest associated with them. The book is as fascinating as a romance but with this difference that we know that every statement within its pages is authentic, that the people who pass before us are not shadowy names, but real flesh and blood personages who have played or are already playing their parts on life's great stage."—*Public Opinion* magazine, April 26, 1890.

Her writings reflected three themes that underscored her interests: history, women's rights and art. She also published her articles in a wide variety of leading national publications of that era. This freelancing surely required tenacity as writing was then still a man's profession. At the same time, it added to her portfolio of accomplishments as an author and put extra money in her pocket. She discussed equal rights and race in *The Chautauquan* magazine in an 1892 article, *"Women in the Treasury Department in Washington."* It told about a black woman who earned $12 per month as a sweeper and a woman auditor who faced a "gauntlet of distrust and opposition." She also combined her interest in history and sewing/embroidery in an article she penned called, *"Dreams in Woven Thread,"* in *The Cosmopolitan* magazine in December 1895. It discussed a variety of antique embellished clothing in a historic exhibit. The next year she wrote *"The Divine Afflatus of the Etruscan Gold-Spinners"*

POINT D'ARGENTAN.

DREAMS IN WOVEN THREAD.

BY MARY F. LOCKWOOD.

ONE of the greatest attractions of the Smithsonian Institution is the exhibit of laces collected and owned by Dr. Thomas Wilson, Curator, Department of Prehistoric Anthropology, United States National Museum.

This collection was at the Atlanta Exposition most appropriately installed in the Woman's building. It is an exhibit fascinating to women,—for of lace they never tire,—and more, it is a handicraft in which the work of the deft fingers of woman alone can be traced from the earliest days of its history to the present time.

This collection, in which Professor Wilson has been engaged for twenty years, does not represent the historical laces of the queens of the world, but it is designed as an historical exhibit of lace about Italy's lost arts in *The Arena* magazine.

Through her efforts and the others in the Woman's National Press Association, women journalists broke through barriers in political coverage on Capitol Hill. The association successfully fought for the rights of women journalists to have seats, set apart for their use, in both houses of Congress—despite the fact that women still couldn't vote. This interesting, obscure fact was noted in *The Writer* magazine in 1889. It also made known that the association had retained "permanent and pleasing headquarters at Willard's Hotel."

Mary had many accomplishments to promote the cause of women as well as encourage interest

Mary at DAR Headquarters. She obviously liked fashion and ornate fabrics, especially given her writings on needlework and design. In photos, she is easily the best dressed of DAR's founders. She never worked as a civil servant, but at the Strathmore Arms and as a long-time author. She may have been the most well off of the founders, too, given her steady earnings from writing and the high volume she produced in books, booklets and articles for magazines and newspapers. Public domain photo courtesy of DAR.

in history, the arts, literature and travel when she wrote a letter to *The Washington Post* during the summer of 1890 that would change history and impact generations of women across the world. Mary spoke about what happened that morning to a reporter for *The Washington Herald,* printed Jan. 28, 1912. She was seated at her desk on a sunny morning at work preparing to give a lecture on "Woman as an Architect" to the upcoming Chicago World's Fair in 1893. Mary had been appointed by President Benjamin Harrison to be on the Lady Managers Board. She paused her work to read a newspaper, which noted that a new organization called the Sons of the American Revolution (SAR) had met in Washington, D.C., and voted to exclude women. She became upset when she read a speech given at the SAR meeting by U.S. Sen. John Sherman (Ohio) in which he said that "women might not have done any fighting, but they kept the farm going; raised the crops that fed the Army, spun the yarn and wove the cloth that clothed the soldiers; looked after the homes and the children; kept the country alive…"

Mary became outraged, even rereading Sherman's address a second time, muttering, "They even helped to the fighting when occasion demanded." She said her mind quickly turned to:

• Mollie Pitcher—the nickname of Mary Ludwig Hays McCauly who carried water to in 1778 American troops during the Battle of Monmouth in New Jersey and stood in to fight after her husband couldn't.

- Deborah Sampson—who disguised herself as a man named Robert Shurtleff, joined the 4th Massachusetts Regiment in 1782, fought as a soldier and earned a military pension.
- The all-woman militia of Pepperill Bridge—who formed in Massachusetts after the men marched off to fight in 1775. The group of 40 dressed in their husbands' clothes, grabbed weapons, guarded a road through Pepperill and captured a group of horsemen who wanted to give aid to the British.

Mary recalled that she couldn't get rid of the thought, "Why should women not now give their work and time to the commemoration of the dames as well as the sires of that splendid struggle for liberty!" It bothered her so much she couldn't continue working on the lecture. "I thought of those brave women of the American Revolution, of whom Sen. Sherman had spoken in his address, and it came to me that surely American was broad and just enough to commemorate the names of heroic woman as well as those of heroic men. For it was all true—women had kept America alive while their husbands and brothers fought for its freedom. They did raise the crops that fed the armies; they did spin the yearn and weave the cloth and clothed the soldiers; they did keep the farms growing, and did take care of the little children; and when they were needed, they even answered the call to arms. Were not the memories of these women as dear to America, then, as the names of the men who fought for her liberty?"

What is fascinating about Mary's description

301

of the events leading up to her writing the famous letter is that two of her three examples of fighting women came from Massachusetts, where her family was located during the Revolutionary War. In fact Pepperill, is located 75 miles from the Smith family's hometown of Whately (97 miles from Plympton). It is certainly possible Mary knew about these acts of brave women assisting in battle from oral histories passed down in her family. Her ties to Massachusetts were very close, especially since her parents were born there.

Mary took to her pen and addressed the American people in her letter to the newspaper. She wrote about patriot Hannah Arnett, asking, *"Where will the Sons and Daughters of the American Revolution place Hannah Arnett?"* After the letter was published on Sunday, July 13, 1890, she received correspondence in Tuesday morning's mail from Miss Mary Desha offering to help organize a society of Daughters of the American Revolution.

"Mrs. Lockwood was the one who sounded the bugle call for us to organize," Desha recalled in 1897.

It snowballed from there as more women came forth to join the effort. Then at 2 p.m. on Oct. 11, 1890 (a date Desha said was chosen to coincide with the discovery of America) during a meeting at Mary's Strathmore Arms, the DAR became a full organization with 18 members— including Mary as historian general.

"The dream I dreamed of preserving and honoring the names of American dames that summer morning when I had read Sen. Sherman's address had been more than realized," Mary said. Her DAR National Number was 27.

The year 1893 saw Mary as busy as ever. She worked with women's rights movement leaders Belva Lockwood (no relation) and Susan B. Anthony in 25th Annual Convention of the National American Woman Suffrage Association. The event was touted to "arouse that divine discontent which shall make women ashamed to remain longer in the attitude of wars in their own country;

Belva Lockwood, above (1880). National Portrait Gallery. Susan B. Anthony (1870). Library of Congress.

to stir the dormant sense of justice which shall make me unwilling to monopolize all power, as if women were not to be trusted..." Mary read her paper during the proceedings, was appointed to the Committee on Courtesies and served on a standing committee for local arrangements.

Mary also contributed to an autographed souvenir

cookbook for the Chicago World's Fair as one of the Lady Managers. The cookbook contained illustrations and copies of the signatures of leading women with over 300 recipes. Some women gave their recipes for bread, soup, fish, sauces, meat, poultry, salad, eggs, cakes, cookies, pickles, etc. Mary's favorite dish and recipe is below.

## Omelet

*Beat four fresh eggs slightly with two tablespoonfuls of cream; season with pepper and salt; put in a tablespoonful of butter in the chafing dish, and when very hot pour in the egg; scrape up rapidly from all parts of the pan the cooked egg, letting the liquid portion follow the knife. It takes from 40 to 60 seconds to cook it, then slip the knife under the left edge and fold the omelet over quickly and lightly. Serve on a hot dish.*

*Mary S. Lockwood*

(As a working woman perhaps Mary preferred this simple dish because she didn't like to cook or it made a convenient meal for someone on the go.)

Mary used her talents in numerous ways in DAR. Among these was serving as the second editor of *American Monthly* for six years (Ellen Hardin Walworth had previously served for two years). Mary's daughter, Lillian (Lily) also worked at the magazine as its business manager. As a magazine editor and author, Mary worked tirelessly to promote the cause of women journalists. In February 1898, she was among the leadership at the two-day congress of the Woman's International Press Association who reorganized the group to include men and change its name to The International Press and Authors' Association. It is not surprising she was elected president of this revamped organization.

Lillian (Lily) Lockwood, *Evening Star*, April, 20, 1907.

*The Evening Star* provided a wonderful glimpse of Mary's world at the Strathmore Arms in February 1895 when it detailed a Woman's National Press Association reception that Mary held there. Upon entering the building, attendees were greeted by red, white and blue decorations draped around the rooms, staircase and railings as well as American flags. "Mrs. Lockwood stood just inside the door of the reception room, gowned in brocade velvet and white satin and lace" as she introduced the arriving women journalists. Their dresses were sumptuously adorned in silver and black brocade, garnet silk, fawn-colored velvet, black lace over tan silk, and blue satin and lace. At lunchtime, the women sat at tables with "banks of blood-red tulips in their center" in a red-color theme as the flags hung around mantels and paintings.

By 1894, Mary moved from the *National Republican*, Strathmore Arms to Nov., 13, 1885. board in a dwelling at 1101 K St. N.W. She was 63 years old. No longer managing the establishment, she still pursued her passions. She wrote many articles that appeared in D.C. newspapers and leading magazines using a popular title back then called *"Pen Pictures."* For example, some of her articles were called *"Pen Pictures of Washington"* and *"Pen Pictures of History."* In the *National Newspaper* on Nov. 23, 1899 was an article, *"Yesterday's in Washington, Pen Pictures of Celebrities of the Past Generation,"* which featured her remembrances of notable people in the nation's capital. She became a popular contributor to that newspaper, also writing articles including *"Stories of the Inaugurals from Washington to McKinley"* in 1901.

Mary also took a leadership role in a new group to organized in 1894 for the various women's clubs in Washington, D.C. It became the District Federation of Women's Clubs. Among its leadership were Mary, Ellen Spencer Mussey and Hannah Sperry (journalist/ assistant editor of the *Washington World*). Among the objectives of this umbrella group was to improve the Girl's Reform School to take better care of and protect women prisoners. It also sought to promote the

education of women in medical and law schools. Another project was working to provide a separate kindergarten system in the public schools.

In 1897, she made sure to insert information about DAR and its headquarters inside the Washington Loan and Trust building

DAR headquarters located in Washington Loan and Trust (left) at 902 F St. (1924). Library of Congress.

on 9th and F streets at the top of the "Societies and Clubs" list in a guidebook she wrote: *"Columbia Guide, Historic and Modern Washington."*

Ever the savvy businesswoman, Mary formed a deal with *The National Tribune* in Washington, D.C., in 1900 to conduct genealogy in a newspaper series called "American Families." The way it worked was that genealogies would be provided for six common surnames printed for families with a colonial official or Revolutionary War soldier in their genealogy. "When a subscriber finds a record that is thought to be that of an ancestor, Mrs. Lockwood will assist in tracing and verifying the genealogy. It will thus be seen that for $1 (the subscription price to the *National Tribune* for one year) the subscriber whose descent comes through any of these six family names, may settle the question of Revolutionary ancestry." This ingenious deal no doubt helped all parties. At this time in her life, she moved to a sunny room at the top floor of The Columbia apartments.

It must have been terribly sad for Mary when her beloved brother Rodney, 74, passed away in April 1902 after being ill for over a year. His pallbearers were former

Rodney B. Smith, from *"History of the Town of Whately, Massachusetts,"* (1899).

employees of his paper bag manufacturing company. Mary and daughter Lillian attended the funeral service in Baltimore where he was buried.

Never one to stay idle, Mary continued to devote herself to DAR, women's issues and writing. In 1906, Mary cowrote *"Story of the Records of D.A.R."* with Emily Lee Sherwood. The dedication read: "To the 50,000 Daughters of the American Revolution this volume is most cordially and sincerely dedicated by the authors, as a labor of love."

Her interests after 1906 expanded to social issues impacting juvenile delinquent boys. She wrote about efforts to rehabilitate boys from 13 to 17 who were in the court system for breaking the law. She served as vice president of the Woman's League of the National Junior Republic, a group to help troubled youths with lodging, food and skills, while increasing public awareness and fundraising. "The true American who believes our form of government to be the best in the world should aid in the work of establishing junior republics in every state, where untrained and unprotected children may be trained to realize their responsibility to their government and learn to serve it honestly and zealously," she wrote. The teens in the programs were assisted in finding foster care and earning money on farms and other jobs. They were also provided with schooling and job skills.

She was esteemed nationwide for her achievements. Yet, one of the most tragic events in Mary's life occurred in 1909. *"Death Comes Suddenly to Washington Woman — Mother Prostrated"*—stated *The Washington Times* on March 14, 1909.

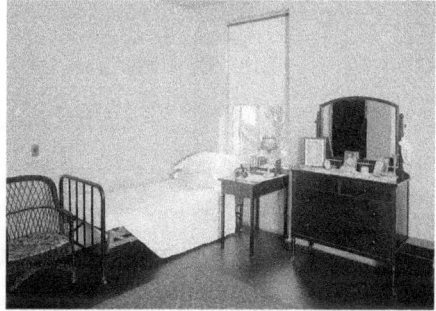

Patient room in the National Homeopathic Hospital in D.C. (1910). Library of Congress.

Lily, about 38 years old, had been working, as usual, as business manager of *American Monthly*. She had been elected to that post continuously for 12 years. The days before her death were among her happiest. Planning to marry soon, she had been celebrating her engagement to prominent attorney Harry W. Van Dyke, who had moved from New York to Washington, D.C.

Suddenly she became stricken with appendicitis. "A few hours before being operated on Thursday, Miss Lockwood was in one of her happiest moods and discussed with her mother their plans for the coming summer," *The Times* noted. She never left the National Homeopathic Hospital and died from complications.

Lily's death "came as a great shock to her many friends" since she had been sick for less than 24 hours. "When the news of her daughter's death came to her, Mrs. Lockwood was completely prostrated and her friends fear she may not survive the shock." The funeral service was officiated Rev. C. Ernest Smith of St. Thomas Episcopal Church in

Lillian (Lily) Lockwood, *American Monthly Magazine.*

a private ceremony "owing to the precarious state of Mrs. Lockwood's health." In attendance at the service held at her apartment at The Columbia were Mary's sister-in-law Rodney's wife and her niece Mrs. George A.C. Christiancy of N.Y. Lily was buried at Rock Creek Cemetery.

"Miss Lockwood was a cheery little body, with clear dark eyes and pretty brown hair, and everybody liked her," stated the *National Tribune* on April 1, 1909. "The sympathy of all will go out to Mrs. Lockwood

[age 77], who is thus left alone in the sunset of life. The relationship between Mary and Lily had been a close one. They both attended events together, shared in the membership in DAR and were active socially. Mary's personality was more extroverted, but they supported each other's work. When Mary wrote the book, *"Yesterdays in Washington,"* published in 1915, she dedicated it to her child.

## DEDICATION

*"To the beloved memory of my daughter LILIAN, whose encouragement sustained me through the years we walked side by side, and who was the inspiration of my work, these volumes are now lovingly inscribed."*

Old age didn't hinder Mary in her fight for women's rights. She remained active in the District of Columbia Federation of Women's Clubs and presented a paper at the public library in January 1914 that she penned called *"History of Women from Ancient Times to the Present."* An entry in a book called *"The Part Taken by Women in American History,"* by Mrs. John A. Logan (1912) discussed Mary in glowing terms. "We look at her with amazement and wonder, when we see this little woman doing so much and still holding all her faculties in calm, leisurely poise. She certainly demonstrates the possibility of combining business with literature, and both with an active sympathy in social reforms, and all with a womanly grace that beautifies every relation of life."

Still busy as ever, Mary switched hats to be a publisher in 1912 of *"Chronicles of the Scott-Irish Settlement in Virginia,"* by Lyman Chalkley.

In 1913, she helped organize and fund a national "Votes for Women" parade of 20,000 women who came to Washington, D.C., in March from every state. Then she participated in it, too. Among a group of eight women (including Belva Lockwood) in the "Pioneer Procession," Mary was driven in line of cars carrying long-time elderly women leaders next to a float for pioneers. She also took charge of

Mary helped organize, fund and participated in this famous D.C., women's march in 1913 over voting rights. *Evening Star,* March 13, 1913.

a six-member committee to organize a march of 400 suffragists from D.C., to Baltimore. Then in April, Mary joined in a march in New York City.

In 1916, she turned her trip to Europe in May 1910 into a 233-page book called *"Afoot and Awheel in Europe."* Ever adventurous despite her age, Mary wrote about this history and wonders she saw in Ireland, Scotland, England, the Netherlands, Germany, France and Spain.

Newspapers throughout the country discussed Mary's activities in DAR and other organizations. As a journalist herself, she often gave interviews to women reporters and spoke to anyone who wanted to hear her views. In October 1920, she participated in an interview in the *Washington Post: "How to be Happy at Ninety."*

"Despite her great age, Mrs. Lockwood, a picturesque figure with snow-white hair, bright blue eyes and a gracious manner, keeps abreast of all the issues of the present, and her great regret is that because she has lived so long in the District, working for every good cause here, she has lost her residence in New York state and cannot vote for [future president Warren] Harding on Nov. 2. Mrs. Lockwood is a lifelong Republican and was a member of the first woman's organization of Republican workers," the *Post* stated, calling her a "devoted adherent of woman suffrage long before it became fashionable or popular."

Mary remained devoted to DAR for the rest of her life. The year 1922 was the first time she was unable to attend Continental Congress due to her poor health. When making addresses at Continental Congress, she didn't speak in a formal way by saying "Ladies," or "Daughters." Instead she called them "Girls" as she stood at the edge of the platform to talk.

Always dressed elegantly and with great flair, Mary in the photo she chose for 1916 adventure travel book *"Afoot and Awheel in Europe."*

Known as the "Little Mother" of DAR, Mary died in a hospital in Plymouth, Mass., on Nov. 9. 1922 at age 91. She had been a patient there for over a year. One obituary noted that she "was blessed with good health almost to the end of her long and useful life." Her funeral was held at the Columbia apartments in Washington, D.C. Her family preferred a quiet affair with only relatives and a few close friends. Continental Hall was closed to the public and flag flown at half-mast from the time her death was announced until after her funeral. Mary was buried in a shared grave with her daughter (where her niece and husband were later interred.)

"Mrs. Lockwood took a prominent part in the fight for equal suffrage, but when the federal Constitution was amended to permit women throughout the land to vote, she never enjoyed the privilege, for she had been a resident of Washington so long she had forfeited the right of franchise," stated *Muskogee Daily Phoenix and Times-Democrat* (Okla.) poignantly in her obituary on Nov. 11, 1922.

She was the last surviving member of the four founders of DAR. A moving tribute to Mary was published by DAR's magazine in December 1922. It ended with the following.

*"Her life all good, no deed for show,*
*No deed to hide,*
*She never caused a tear to flow*
*Save when she died."*

# Author Noël-Marie Fletcher

Noël-Marie Fletcher is a journalist/photographer in Washington, D.C. She is a member of the Daughters of the American Revolution and the Descendants of the Founders of New Jersey.

She attributes her zest for life, analytical abilities, love of adventure and creativity to her unique fusion of ancestors. Her paternal relatives came to America from England, Scotland and Wales as colonists in New Jersey, Pennsylvania, Maryland and Virginia. Many fought as patriots during the Revolutionary War to help establish the United States of America. She is half-Hispanic. Her maternal family left Spain for the New World and settled near Santa Fe, N.M. Her Perea family members were among the earliest Hispanics to serve in the U.S. Congress (Francisco Perea, Jose Francisco Chaves, and Pedro Perea). The Pereas were important community leaders under three flags (Spain, Mexico and the United States) and leading business entrepreneurs who helped found the Santa Fe Trail.

Noël-Marie has lived in Hong Kong, Beijing, and Germany (Nuremberg, Berlin) with a stint in Switzerland. She speaks Spanish, Mandarin Chinese and French. She is the author of over six fiction and nonfiction books. Her autobiographical tale *"My Time in Another World: Experiences as a Foreign Correspondent in China"* won 1st place in 2021 in the in the National Federation of Press Women's at-large competition for autobiography/memoir.

Her interests as a writer include history, journalism and biographies of women. She also creates books that blend her love of nature and animals with her photos and writing. She founded Fletcher & Co. Publishers as an outlet for creative writing, illustrations and photography.

*9781941184387*